MznLnx

Missing Links Exam Preps

Exam Prep for

Applied Calculus

Tan, 6th Edition

The MznLnx Exam Prep is your link from the texbook and lecture to your exams.
The MznLnx Exam Preps are unauthorized and comprehensive reviews of your textbooks.

All material provided by MznLnx and Rico Publications (c) 2010
Textbook publishers and textbook authors do not particpate in or contribute to these reviews.

MznLnx

Rico
Publications

Exam Prep for Applied Calculus
6th Edition
Tan

Publisher: Raymond Houge
Assistant Editor: Michael Rouger
Text and Cover Designer: Lisa Buckner
Marketing Manager: Sara Swagger
Project Manager, Editorial Production: Jerry Emerson
Art Director: Vernon Lowerui

Product Manager: Dave Mason
Editorial Assitant: Rachel Guzmanji
Pedagogy: Debra Long
Cover Image: Jim Reed/Getty Images
Text and Cover Printer: City Printing, Inc.
Compositor: Media Mix, Inc.

(c) 2010 Rico Publications
ALL RIGHTS RESERVED. No part of this work covered by the copyright may be reproduced or used in any form or by an means--graphic, electronic, or mechanical, including photocopying, recording, taping, Web distribution, information storage, and retrieval systems, or in any other manner--without the written permission of the publisher.

Printed in the United States
ISBN:

For more information about our products, contact us at:
Dave.Mason@RicoPublications.com

For permission to use material from this text or product, submit a request online to:
Dave.Mason@RicoPublications.com

Contents

CHAPTER 1
Preliminaries 1

CHAPTER 2
Functions, Limits, and the Derivative 7

CHAPTER 3
Differentiation 21

CHAPTER 4
Applications of the Derivative 30

CHAPTER 5
Exponential and Logarithmic Functions 39

CHAPTER 6
Integration 47

CHAPTER 7
Additional Topics in Integration 57

CHAPTER 8
Calculus of Several Variables 60

CHAPTER 9
Differential Equations 72

CHAPTER 10
Probability and Calculus 77

CHAPTER 11
Taylor Polynomials and Infinite Series 83

CHAPTER 12
Trigonometric Functions 92

ANSWER KEY 100

TO THE STUDENT

COMPREHENSIVE

The *MznLnx* Exam Prep series is designed to help you pass your exams. Editors at MznLnx review your textbooks and then prepare these practice exams to help you master the textbook material. Unlike study guides, workbooks, and practice tests provided by the texbook publisher and textbook authors, *MznLnx* gives you **all** of the material in each chapter in exam form, not just samples, so you can be sure to nail your exam.

MECHANICAL

The MznLnx Exam Prep series creates exams that will help you learn the subject matter as well as test you on your understanding. Each question is designed to help you master the concept. Just working through the exams, you gain an understanding of the subject--its a simple mechanical process that produces success.

INTEGRATED STUDY GUIDE AND REVIEW

MznLnx is not just a set of exams designed to test you, its also a comprehensive review of the subject content. Each exam question is also a review of the concept, making sure that you will get the answer correct without having to go to other sources of material. You learn as you go! Its the easiest way to pass an exam.

HUMOR

Studying can be tedious and dry. MznLnx's instructional design includes moderate humor within the exam questions on occassion, to break the tedium and revitalize the brain

Chapter 1. Preliminaries

1. In mathematics and its applications, a _____ system is a system for assigning an n-tuple of numbers or scalars to each point in an n-dimensional space. This concept is part of the theory of manifolds. 'Scalars' in many cases means real numbers, but, depending on context, can mean complex numbers or elements of some other commutative ring.
   a. Spherical coordinate system
   b. Cylindrical coordinate system
   c. 15 theorem
   d. Coordinate

2. Integration is an important concept in mathematics, specifically in the field of calculus and, more broadly, mathematical analysis. Given a function f of a real variable x and an interval [a, b] of the real line, the _____

$$\int_a^b f(x)\,dx,$$

is defined informally to be the net signed area of the region in the xy-plane bounded by the graph of f, the x-axis, and the vertical lines x = a and x = b.

The term '_____' may also refer to the notion of antiderivative, a function F whose derivative is the given function f.

   a. Integral test for convergence
   b. Indefinite integral
   c. Integrand
   d. Integral

3. A _____ is an algebraic equation in which each term is either a constant or the product of a constant and (the first power of) a single variable. Linear equations can have one, two, three or more variables. Linear equations occur with great regularity in applied mathematics.
   a. Linear equation
   b. Quartic function
   c. Quadratic formula
   d. Cubic function

4. Cantor defined two kinds of _____ numbers, the ordinal numbers and the cardinal numbers. Ordinal numbers may be identified with well-ordered sets, or counting carried on to any stopping point, including points after an _____ number have already been counted. Generalizing finite and the ordinary _____ sequences which are maps from the positive integers leads to mappings from ordinal numbers, and transfinite sequences.

a. Infinite
b. AUSM
c. ACTRAN
d. ALGOR

5. In metric topology and related fields of mathematics, a set U is called _____ if, intuitively speaking, starting from any point x in U one can move by a small amount in any direction and still be in the set U. In other words, the distance between any point x in U and the edge of U is always greater than zero.

As an example, consider the _____ interval (0, 1) consisting of all real numbers x with 0 < x < 1. Here, the topology is the usual topology on the real line. We can look at this in two ways.

a. AUSM
b. Open
c. ALGOR
d. ACTRAN

6. In mathematics, the _____ (or modulus) of a real number is its numerical value without regard to its sign. So, for example, 3 is the _____ of both 3 and −3.

The _____ of a number a is denoted by $|a|$.

a. ACTRAN
b. Exponential function
c. Area hyperbolic functions
d. Absolute value

7. A quadratic equation with real or complex coefficients has two solutions (or roots), not necessarily distinct, which may or may not be real, given by the _____:

$$\frac{-b \pm \sqrt{b^2 - 4ac}}{2a}$$

Example discriminant signsâ− <0: $x^2 + \frac{1}{2}$â− =0: $-\frac{4}{3}x^2 + \frac{4}{3}x - \frac{1}{3}$â− >0: $\frac{3}{2}x^2 + \frac{1}{2}x - \frac{4}{3}$

In the above formula, the expression underneath the square root sign

$$D = b^2 - 4ac,$$

is called the discriminant of the quadratic equation.

A quadratic equation with real coefficients can have either one or two distinct real roots, or two distinct complex roots. In this case the discriminant determines the number and nature of the roots.

- a. Linear equation
- b. Cubic function
- c. Quartic function
- d. Quadratic formula

8. In mathematics, the _____ is used to determine each point uniquely in a plane through two numbers, usually called the x-coordinate or abscissa and the y-coordinate or ordinate of the point. To define the coordinates, two perpendicular directed lines, are specified, as well as the unit length, which is marked off on the two axes Cartesian coordinate systems are also used in space and in higher dimensions.
- a. 15 theorem
- b. Coordinate
- c. Cylindrical coordinate system
- d. Cartesian coordinate system

9. In computer science and information science, _____ could also be a method or an algorithm. Again, an example will illustrate: There are systems of counting, as with Roman numerals, and various systems for filing papers, or catalogues, and various library systems, of which the Dewey Decimal _____ is an example. This still fits with the definition of components which are connected together (in this case in order to facilitate the flow of information.)
- a. System
- b. 15 theorem
- c. BDDC
- d. BIBO stability

10. _____ is used to describe the steepness, incline, gradient, or grade of a straight line. A higher _____ value indicates a steeper incline. The _____ is defined as the ratio of the 'rise' divided by the 'run' between two points on a line, or in other words, the ratio of the altitude change to the horizontal distance between any two points on the line.

a. 15 theorem
b. Y-intercept
c. Sequence
d. Slope

11. If a function has an integral, it is said to be integrable. The function for which the integral is calculated is called the _____. The region over which a function is being integrated is called the domain of integration.
a. Order of integration
b. Integral test for convergence
c. Integration by parts
d. Integrand

12. In calculus, a _____ is either of the two limits of a function f(x) of a real variable x as x approaches a specified point either from below or from above. One should write either:

$$\lim_{x \to a^+} f(x) \text{ or } \lim_{x \downarrow a} f(x)$$

for the limit as x decreases in value approaching a (x approaches a 'from above' or 'from the right'), and similarly

$$\lim_{x \to a^-} f(x) \text{ or } \lim_{x \uparrow a} f(x)$$

for the limit as x increases in value approaching a (x approaches a 'from below' or 'from the left'.)

The two one-sided limits exist and are equal if and only if the limit of f(x) as x approaches a exists.

a. AUSM
b. ACTRAN
c. ALGOR
d. One-sided limit

13. In mathematics, the concept of a '_____' is used to describe the behavior of a function as its argument or input either 'gets close' to some point, or as the argument becomes arbitrarily large; or the behavior of a sequence's elements as their index increases indefinitely. Limits are used in calculus and other branches of mathematical analysis to define derivatives and continuity.

In formulas, _____ is usually abbreviated as lim

a. 15 theorem
b. BIBO stability
c. Limit
d. BDDC

14. This article will state and prove the _____ for differentiation, and then use it to prove these two formulas.

The _____ for differentiation states that for every natural number n, the derivative of $f(x) = x^n$ is $f'(x) = nx^{n-1}$, that is,

$$(x^n)' = nx^{n-1}.$$

The _____ for integration

$$\int x^n \, dx = \frac{x^{n+1}}{n+1} + C$$

for natural n is then an easy consequence. One just needs to take the derivative of this equality and use the _____ and linearity of differentiation on the right-hand side.

a. Test for Divergence
b. Leibniz rule
c. Power Rule
d. Functional integration

15. A _____ officer is an officer of high military rank. The term or equivalent is used by nearly every country in the world. _____ can be used as a generic term for all grades of _____ officer, or it can specifically refer to a single rank that is just called _____.
a. General
b. 15 theorem
c. BIBO stability
d. BDDC

16. In numerical analysis, _____ constitutes a broad family of algorithms for calculating the numerical value of a definite integral, and by extension, the term is also sometimes used to describe the numerical solution of differential equations The term numerical quadrature is more or less a synonym for _____, especially as applied to one-dimensional integrals.

a. Multigrid method
b. Galerkin methods
c. Meshfree methods
d. Numerical integration

Chapter 2. Functions, Limits, and the Derivative

1. In calculus, a method called _____ can be applied to implicitly defined functions. This method is an application of the chain rule allowing one to calculate the derivative of a function given implicitly.

    As explained in the introduction, y can be given as a function of x implicitly rather than explicitly. When we have an equation R(x,y) = 0, we may be able to solve it for y and then differentiate. However, sometimes it is simpler to differentiate R(x,y) with respect to x and then solve for dy / dx.

    a. Automatic differentiation
    b. Ordinary differential equation
    c. Implicit function
    d. Implicit differentiation

2. In mathematics, the _____ of a function is the set of all 'output' values produced by that function. Sometimes it is called the image, or more precisely, the image of the domain of the function. If a function is a surjection then its _____ is equal to its codomain.
    a. Surjective
    b. Constant function
    c. Piecewise-defined function
    d. Range

3. In calculus, a branch of mathematics, the _____ is a measurement of how a function changes when its input changes. Loosely speaking, a _____ can be thought of as how much a quantity is changing at some given point. For example, the _____ of the position (or distance) of a vehicle with respect to time is the instantaneous velocity (respectively, instantaneous speed) at which the vehicle is traveling.

    The process of finding a _____ is called differentiation. The fundamental theorem of calculus states that differentiation is the reverse process to integration.

    a. Derivative
    b. Semi-differentiability
    c. Bounded function
    d. Stationary phase approximation

4. In mathematics, the _____ (or replacement set) of a given function is the set of 'input' values for which the function is defined. For instance, the _____ of cosine would be all real numbers, while the _____ of the square root would be only numbers greater than or equal to 0 (ignoring complex numbers in both cases.) In a representation of a function in a xy Cartesian coordinate system, the _____ is represented on the x axis (or abscissa.)

a. BDDC
b. 15 theorem
c. Domain
d. BIBO stability

5. The terms '_____' and 'independent variable' are used in similar but subtly different ways in mathematics and statistics as part of the standard terminology in those subjects. They are used to distinguish between two types of quantities being considered, separating them into those available at the start of a process and those being created by it, where the latter (dependent variables) are dependent on the former (independent variables.)

In traditional calculus, a function is defined as a relation between two terms called variables because their values vary.

a. BDDC
b. 15 theorem
c. BIBO stability
d. Dependent variable

6. The terms 'dependent variable' and '_____' are used in similar but subtly different ways in mathematics and statistics as part of the standard terminology in those subjects. They are used to distinguish between two types of quantities being considered, separating them into those available at the start of a process and those being created by it, where the latter (dependent variables) are dependent on the former (independent variables.)

In traditional calculus, a function is defined as a relation between two terms called variables because their values vary.

a. AUSM
b. ALGOR
c. ACTRAN
d. Independent variable

7. In calculus, an _____ is the limit of a definite integral as an endpoint of the interval of integration approaches either a specified real number or ∞ or −∞ or, in some cases, as both endpoints approach limits.

Specifically, an _____ is a limit of the form

$$\lim_{b \to \infty} \int_a^b f(x)\, dx, \qquad \lim_{a \to -\infty} \int_a^b f(x)\, dx,$$

or of the form

$$\lim_{c \to b^-} \int_a^c f(x)\,dx, \quad \lim_{c \to a^+} \int_c^b f(x)\,dx,$$

in which one takes a limit in one or the other (or sometimes both) endpoints. Improper integrals may also occur at an interior point of the domain of integration, or at multiple such points.

a. AUSM
b. ALGOR
c. ACTRAN
d. Improper integral

8. Integration is an important concept in mathematics, specifically in the field of calculus and, more broadly, mathematical analysis. Given a function f of a real variable x and an interval [a, b] of the real line, the _____

$$\int_a^b f(x)\,dx,$$

is defined informally to be the net signed area of the region in the xy-plane bounded by the graph of f, the x-axis, and the vertical lines x = a and x = b.

The term '_____' may also refer to the notion of antiderivative, a function F whose derivative is the given function f.

a. Integral test for convergence
b. Integral
c. Indefinite integral
d. Integrand

9. In calculus and other branches of mathematical analysis, an _____ is an algebraic expression obtained in the context of limits. Limits involving algebraic operations are often performed by replacing subexpressions by their limits; if the expression obtained after this substitution does not give enough information to determine the original limit, it is known as an _____. The indeterminate forms include 0^0, $0/0$, 1^∞, $\infty - \infty$, ∞/∞, $0 \times \infty$, and ∞^0.

a. ACTRAN
b. AUSM
c. ALGOR
d. Indeterminate form

10. In mathematics, the _____ is a conic section, the intersection of a right circular conical surface and a plane parallel to a generating straight line of that surface. Given a point (the focus) and a line (the directrix) that lie in a plane, the locus of points in that plane that are equidistant to them is a _____.

A particular case arises when the plane is tangent to the conical surface of a circle.

a. BIBO stability
b. Parabola
c. 15 theorem
d. BDDC

11. In mathematics, a _____ is a function whose definition is dependent on the value of the independent variable. Mathematically, a real-valued function f of a real variable x is a relationship whose definition is given differently on disjoint subsets of its domain

The word piecewise is also used to describe any property of a _____ that holds for each piece but may not hold for the whole domain of the function.

a. Surjective
b. Range
c. Constant function
d. Piecewise-defined function

12. In infinitesimal calculus, a _____ is traditionally an infinitesimally small change in a variable. For example, if x is a variable, then a change in the value of x is often denoted Δx (or δx when this change is considered to be small.) The _____ dx represents such a change, but is infinitely small.

a. Dirichlet integral
b. Local maximum
c. The Method of Mechanical Theorems
d. Differential

Chapter 2. Functions, Limits, and the Derivative

13. In mathematics, the simplest case of _____ refers to the study of problems in which one seeks to minimize or maximize a real function by systematically choosing the values of real or integer variables from within an allowed set. This (a scalar real valued objective function) is actually a small subset of this field which comprises a large area of applied mathematics and generalizes to study of means to obtain 'best available' values of some objective function given a defined domain where the elaboration is on the types of functions and the conditions and nature of the objects in the problem domain.

The first _____ technique, which is known as steepest descent, goes back to Gauss.

a. AUSM
b. Optimization
c. ACTRAN
d. ALGOR

14. _____ is a type of motion in which the velocity of an object changes equal amounts in equal time periods. An example of an object having _____ would be a ball rolling down a ramp. The object picks up velocity as it goes down the ramp with equal changes in time.

a. ALGOR
b. Uniform Acceleration
c. ACTRAN
d. AUSM

15. In mathematics, a _____ represents the application of one function to the results of another. For instance, the functions f: X → Y and g: Y → Z can be composed by first computing f(x) and then applying a function g to the output of f(x.)

Thus one obtains a function g ∘ f: X → Z defined by (g ∘ f)(x) = g(f(x)) for all x in X. The notation g ∘ f is read as 'g circle f', or 'g composed with f', 'g after f', 'g following f', or just 'g of f'.

a. Surjective
b. Constant function
c. Piecewise-defined function
d. Composite function

16. Just as the definite integral of a positive function of one variable represents the area of the region between the graph of the function and the x-axis, the _____ of a positive function of two variables represents the volume of the region between the surface defined by the function (on the three dimensional Cartesian plane where z = f(x,y)) and the plane which contains its domain. (Note that the same volume can be obtained via the triple integral -- the integral of a function in three variables -- of the constant function f(x, y, z) = 1 over the above-mentioned region between the surface and the plane.) If there are more variables, a multiple integral will yield hypervolumes of multi-dimensional functions.

Chapter 2. Functions, Limits, and the Derivative

   a. Constant of integration
   b. Double integral
   c. Risch algorithm
   d. Trigonometric substitution

17. In probability theory and statistics, the _____ (or expectation value or mean and for continuous random variables with a density function it is the probability density -weighted integral of the possible values.

The term '_____' can be misleading.

   a. ALGOR
   b. AUSM
   c. ACTRAN
   d. Expected value

18. The _____ of a quantity whose value decreases with time is the interval required for the quantity to decay to half of its initial value. The concept originated in describing how long it takes atoms to undergo radioactive decay but also applies in a wide variety of other situations.

The term '_____' dates to 1907.

   a. BIBO stability
   b. 15 theorem
   c. Half-life
   d. BDDC

19. Cantor defined two kinds of _____ numbers, the ordinal numbers and the cardinal numbers. Ordinal numbers may be identified with well-ordered sets, or counting carried on to any stopping point, including points after an _____ number have already been counted. Generalizing finite and the ordinary _____ sequences which are maps from the positive integers leads to mappings from ordinal numbers, and transfinite sequences.
   a. AUSM
   b. ALGOR
   c. Infinite
   d. ACTRAN

20. The terms of the series are often produced according to a certain rule, such as by a formula, by an algorithm, by a sequence of measurements, or even by a random number generator. As there are an infinite number of terms, this notion is often called an _____. Unlike finite summations, series need tools from mathematical analysis to be fully understood and manipulated.
   a. Integration by substitution
   b. Extreme value
   c. Extreme Value Theorem
   d. Infinite series

21. A _____, in mathematics, is a polynomial function of the form $f(x) = ax^2 + bx + c$, where $a \neq 0$. The graph of a _____ is a parabola whose major axis is parallel to the y-axis.

The expression $ax^2 + bx + c$ in the definition of a _____ is a polynomial of degree 2 or a 2nd degree polynomial, because the highest exponent of x is 2.

   a. Quadratic function
   b. Discriminant
   c. Resultant
   d. Leading coefficient

22. In mathematics, a _____ is any function which can be written as the ratio of two polynomial functions.

$$y = \frac{x^2 - 3x - 2}{x^2 - 4}$$

In the case of one variable, x, a _____ is a function of the form

$$f(x) = \frac{P(x)}{Q(x)}$$

where P and Q are polynomial function in x and Q is not the zero polynomial. The domain of f is the set of all points x for which the denominator Q(x) is not zero.

   a. BIBO stability
   b. BDDC
   c. 15 theorem
   d. Rational function

23. In mathematics, a (topological) _____ is defined as follows: let I be an interval of real numbers (i.e. a non-empty connected subset of $\mathbb{R}$); then a _____ γ is a continuous mapping $\gamma : I \to X$, where X is a topological space. The _____ γ is said to be simple if it is injective, i.e. if for all x, y in I, we have $\gamma(x) = \gamma(y) \implies x = y$. If I is a closed bounded interval $[a, b]$, we also allow the possibility $\gamma(a) = \gamma(b)$ (this convention makes it possible to talk about closed simple _____.)

a. Curve
b. Closed curve
c. Prolate cycloid
d. Tractrix

24. In acoustics and telecommunication, a _____ of a wave is a component frequency of the signal that is an integer multiple of the fundamental frequency. For example, if the fundamental frequency is f, the harmonics have frequencies f, 2f, 3f, 4f, etc. The harmonics have the property that they are all periodic at the fundamental frequency, therefore the sum of harmonics is also periodic at that frequency.

a. BIBO stability
b. 15 theorem
c. BDDC
d. Harmonic

25. In mathematics, the _____ is the infinite series

$$\sum_{k=1}^{\infty} \frac{1}{k} = 1 + \frac{1}{2} + \frac{1}{3} + \frac{1}{4} + \cdots.$$

Its name derives from the concept of overtones, or harmonics, in music: the wavelengths of the overtones of a vibrating string are 1/2, 1/3, 1/4, etc., of the string's fundamental wavelength. Every term of the series after the first is the harmonic mean of the neighboring terms; the term harmonic mean likewise derives from music.

The _____ diverges to infinity, albeit rather slowly (the first 10^{43} terms sum to less than 100 .)

a. Harmonic series
b. BIBO stability
c. 15 theorem
d. BDDC

Chapter 2. Functions, Limits, and the Derivative

26. In mathematics, the concept of a '_____' is used to describe the behavior of a function as its argument or input either 'gets close' to some point, or as the argument becomes arbitrarily large; or the behavior of a sequence's elements as their index increases indefinitely. Limits are used in calculus and other branches of mathematical analysis to define derivatives and continuity.

In formulas, _____ is usually abbreviated as lim

   a. Limit
   b. BIBO stability
   c. 15 theorem
   d. BDDC

27. In geometry, the _____ (or simply the tangent) to a curve at a given point is the straight line that 'just touches' the curve at that point (in the sense explained more precisely below.) As it passes through the point of tangency, the _____ is 'going in the same direction' as the curve, and in this sense it is the best straight-line approximation to the curve at that point. The same definition applies to space curves and curves in n-dimensional Euclidean space.

   a. Lie derivative
   b. Minimal surface
   c. North pole
   d. Tangent line

28. In physics, _____ is defined as the rate of change of position. it is vector physical quantity; both speed and direction are required to define it. In the SI (metric) system, it is measured in meters per second: (m/s) or ms^{-1}.

   a. 15 theorem
   b. Velocity
   c. BIBO stability
   d. BDDC

29. An _____ of a real-valued function y = f(x) is a curve which describes the behavior of f as either x or y tends to infinity.

In other words, as one moves along the graph of f(x) in some direction, the distance between it and the _____ eventually becomes smaller than any distance that one may specify.

   a. ALGOR
   b. AUSM
   c. ACTRAN
   d. Asymptote

Chapter 2. Functions, Limits, and the Derivative

30. Suppose f is a function. Then the line y = a is a _____ for f if

$$\lim_{x \to \infty} f(x) = a \quad \text{or} \quad \lim_{x \to -\infty} f(x) = a.$$

Intuitively, this means that f(x) can be made as close as desired to a by making x big enough. How big is big enough depends on how close one wishes to make f(x) to a.

   a. Third derivative
   b. Horizontal asymptote
   c. Mountain pass theorem
   d. Second derivative

31. In calculus, the _____ is a formula used to find the derivatives of products of functions. It may be stated thus:

$$(f \cdot g)' = f' \cdot g + f \cdot g'$$

or in the Leibniz notation thus:

$$\frac{d}{dx}(u \cdot v) = u \cdot \frac{dv}{dx} + v \cdot \frac{du}{dx}.$$

Discovery of this rule is credited to Gottfried Leibniz, who demonstrated it using differentials. Here is Leibniz's argument: Let u and v be two differentiable functions of x.

   a. Quotient Rule
   b. Differentiation rules
   c. Constant factor rule in differentiation
   d. Product Rule

32. In calculus, a _____ is either of the two limits of a function f(x) of a real variable x as x approaches a specified point either from below or from above. One should write either:

$$\lim_{x \to a^+} f(x) \quad \text{or} \quad \lim_{x \downarrow a} f(x)$$

for the limit as x decreases in value approaching a (x approaches a 'from above' or 'from the right'), and similarly

$$\lim_{x \to a^-} f(x) \quad \text{or} \quad \lim_{x \uparrow a} f(x)$$

Chapter 2. Functions, Limits, and the Derivative

for the limit as x increases in value approaching a (x approaches a 'from below' or 'from the left'.)

The two one-sided limits exist and are equal if and only if the limit of f(x) as x approaches a exists.

a. ACTRAN
b. ALGOR
c. AUSM
d. One-sided limit

33. A quadratic equation with real or complex coefficients has two solutions (or roots), not necessarily distinct, which may or may not be real, given by the _____:

$$\frac{-b \pm \sqrt{b^2 - 4ac}}{2a}$$

Example discriminant signsâ– <0: $x^2+\frac{1}{2}$â– =0: $-\frac{4}{3}x^2+\frac{4}{3}x-\frac{1}{3}$â– >0: $\frac{3}{2}x^2+\frac{1}{2}x-\frac{4}{3}$

In the above formula, the expression underneath the square root sign

$$D = b^2 - 4ac,$$

is called the discriminant of the quadratic equation.

A quadratic equation with real coefficients can have either one or two distinct real roots, or two distinct complex roots. In this case the discriminant determines the number and nature of the roots.

a. Quartic function
b. Quadratic formula
c. Cubic function
d. Linear equation

34. In mathematics, a _____ is a function for which, intuitively, small changes in the input result in small changes in the output. Otherwise, a function is said to be discontinuous. A _____ with a continuous inverse function is called bicontinuous. An intuitive though imprecise (and inexact) idea of continuity is given by the common statement that a _____ is a function whose graph can be drawn without lifting the chalk from the blackboard.

Chapter 2. Functions, Limits, and the Derivative

  a. Hyperbolic angle
  b. Continuous function
  c. Binomial series
  d. Visual Calculus

35. A _____ is a statement of the meaning of a word or phrase. The term to be defined is known as the definiendum . The words which define it are known as the definiens .
  a. BDDC
  b. BIBO stability
  c. Definition
  d. 15 theorem

36. In mathematical analysis, the _____ states that for each value between the least upper bound and greatest lower bound of the image of a continuous function there is a corresponding value in its domain mapping to the original. _____

- Version I. The _____ states the following: If the function y = f(x) is continuous on the interval [a, b], and u is a number between f(a) and f(b), then there is a c ∈ [a, b] such that f(c) = u.

- Version II. Suppose that I is an interval [a, b] in the real numbers R and that f : I → R is a continuous function. Then the image set f(I) is also an interval, and either it contains [f(a), f(b)], or it contains [f(b), f(a)]; that is,

    f(I) ⊇ [f(a), f(b)], or f(I) ⊇ [f(b), f(a)].

It is frequently stated in the following equivalent form: Suppose that f : [a, b] → R is continuous and that u is a real number satisfying f(a) < u < f(b) or f(a) > u > f(b.) Then for some c ∈ [a, b], f(c) = u.

This captures an intuitive property of continuous functions: given f continuous on [1, 2], if f(1) = 3 and f(2) = 5 then f must take the value 4 somewhere between 1 and 2.

  a. AUSM
  b. ALGOR
  c. ACTRAN
  d. Intermediate Value Theorem

37. In geometry, _____ is the division of something into two equal or congruent parts, usually by a line, which is then called a bisector. The most often considered types of bisectors are segment bisectors and angle bisectors. _____ of a line segment using a compass and ruler _____ of an angle using a compass and ruler Line DE bisects line AB at D, line EF is a perpendicular bisector of segment AD at C and the interior bisector of right angle AED

A line segment bisector passes through the midpoint of the segment.

a. BDDC
b. BIBO stability
c. 15 theorem
d. Bisection

38. A _____ of a curve is a line that (locally) intersects two points on the curve. The word secant comes from the Latin secare, for to cut.

It can be used to approximate the tangent to a curve, at some point P. If the secant to a curve is defined by two points, P and Q, with P fixed and Q variable, as Q approaches P along the curve, the direction of the secant approaches that of the tangent at P, assuming there is just one.

a. Curve
b. Secant line
c. Kappa curve
d. Witch of Agnesi

39. _____ is used to describe the steepness, incline, gradient, or grade of a straight line. A higher _____ value indicates a steeper incline. The _____ is defined as the ratio of the 'rise' divided by the 'run' between two points on a line, or in other words, the ratio of the altitude change to the horizontal distance between any two points on the line.

a. Y-intercept
b. Sequence
c. 15 theorem
d. Slope

40. The function difference divided by the point difference is known as the _____, it is also known as Newton's quotient):

$$\frac{\Delta F(P)}{\Delta P} = \frac{F(P+\Delta P) - F(P)}{\Delta P} = \frac{\nabla F(P+\Delta P)}{\Delta P}.$$

Chapter 2. Functions, Limits, and the Derivative

If ΔP is infinitesimal, then the _____ is a derivative, otherwise it is a divided difference:

$$\text{If } |\Delta P| = iota: \quad \frac{\Delta F(P)}{\Delta P} = \frac{dF(P)}{dP} = F'(P) = G(P);$$

$$\text{If } |\Delta P| > iota: \quad \frac{\Delta F(P)}{\Delta P} = \frac{DF(P)}{DP} = F[P, P + \Delta P].$$

Regardless if ΔP is infinitesimal or finite, there is (at least--in the case of the derivative--theoretically) a point range, where the boundaries are P ± (.5)ΔP (depending on the orientation--ΔF(P), δF(P) or ∇F(P)):

    LB = Lower Boundary; UB = Upper Boundary;

Anyone familiar with derivatives knows that they can be regarded as functions themselves, harboring their own derivatives. Thus each function is home to sequential degrees ('higher orders') of derivation, or differentiation. This property can be generalized to all difference quotients. As this sequencing requires a corresponding boundary splintering, it is practical to break up the point range into smaller, equi-sized sections, with each section being marked by an intermediary point ('P_i'), where LB = P_0 and UB = P_{A_n}, the nth point, equaling the degree/order:

LB = P_0 = P_0 + 0Δ_1P = P_{A_n} - (Åf-0)Δ_1P; P_1 = P_0 + 1Δ_1P = P_{A_n} - (Åf-1)Δ_1P; P_2 = P_0 + 2Δ_1P = P_{A_n} - (Åf-2)Δ_1P; P_3 = P_0 + 3Δ_1P = P_{A_n} - (Åf-3)Δ_1P; ↓↓↓↓ P_{A_n-3} = P_0 + (Åf-3)Δ_1P = P_{A_n} - 3Δ_1P; P_{A_n-2} = P_0 + (Åf-2)Δ_1P = P_{A_n} - 2Δ_1P; P_{A_n-1} = P_0 + (Åf-1)Δ_1P = P_{A_n} - 1Δ_1P; UB = P_{A_n-0} = P_0 + (Åf-0)Δ_1P = P_{A_n} - 0Δ_1P = P_{A_n};

ΔP = Δ_1P = P_1 - P_0 = P_2 - P_1 = P_3 - P_2 = ...

    a. Continuously differentiable
    b. Directional derivative
    c. Notation for differentiation
    d. Difference quotient

Chapter 3. Differentiation 21

1. This article will state and prove the _____ for differentiation, and then use it to prove these two formulas.

The _____ for differentiation states that for every natural number n, the derivative of $f(x) = x^n$ is $f'(x) = nx^{n-1}$, that is,

$$(x^n)' = nx^{n-1}.$$

The _____ for integration

$$\int x^n \, dx = \frac{x^{n+1}}{n+1} + C$$

for natural n is then an easy consequence. One just needs to take the derivative of this equality and use the _____ and linearity of differentiation on the right-hand side.

   a. Leibniz rule
   b. Functional integration
   c. Test for Divergence
   d. Power Rule

2. In calculus, a branch of mathematics, the _____ is a measurement of how a function changes when its input changes. Loosely speaking, a _____ can be thought of as how much a quantity is changing at some given point. For example, the _____ of the position (or distance) of a vehicle with respect to time is the instantaneous velocity (respectively, instantaneous speed) at which the vehicle is traveling.

The process of finding a _____ is called differentiation. The fundamental theorem of calculus states that differentiation is the reverse process to integration.

   a. Semi-differentiability
   b. Stationary phase approximation
   c. Bounded function
   d. Derivative

3. _____ is a type of motion in which the velocity of an object changes equal amounts in equal time periods. An example of an object having _____ would be a ball rolling down a ramp. The object picks up velocity as it goes down the ramp with equal changes in time.

a. ALGOR
b. ACTRAN
c. AUSM
d. Uniform Acceleration

4. In calculus, the _____ is a formula used to find the derivatives of products of functions. It may be stated thus:

$$(f \cdot g)' = f' \cdot g + f \cdot g'$$

or in the Leibniz notation thus:

$$\frac{d}{dx}(u \cdot v) = u \cdot \frac{dv}{dx} + v \cdot \frac{du}{dx}.$$

Discovery of this rule is credited to Gottfried Leibniz, who demonstrated it using differentials. Here is Leibniz's argument: Let u and v be two differentiable functions of x.

a. Product Rule
b. Differentiation rules
c. Quotient Rule
d. Constant factor rule in differentiation

5. In calculus, the _____ is a method of finding the derivative of a function that is the quotient of two other functions for which derivatives exist.

If the function one wishes to differentiate, f(x), can be written as

$$f(x) = \frac{g(x)}{h(x)}$$

and h(x) ≠ 0, then the rule states that the derivative of g(x) / h(x) is equal to:

$$\frac{d}{dx}f(x) = f'(x) = \frac{g'(x)h(x) - g(x)h'(x)}{[h(x)]^2}.$$

Chapter 3. Differentiation

Or, more precisely, if all x in some open set containing the number a satisfy h(x) ≠ 0; and g'(a) and h'(a) both exist; then, f'(a) exists as well and:

$$f'(a) = \frac{g'(a)h(a) - g(a)h'(a)}{[h(a)]^2}.$$

The derivative of (4x − 2) / (x² + 1) is:

$$\frac{d}{dx}\left[\frac{(4x-2)}{x^2+1}\right] = \frac{(x^2+1)(4) - (4x-2)(2x)}{(x^2+1)^2}$$

$$= \frac{(4x^2+4) - (8x^2-4x)}{(x^2+1)^2} = \frac{-4x^2+4x+4}{(x^2+1)^2}$$

In the example above, the choices

g(x) = 4x − 2
h(x) = x² + 1

were made. Analogously, the derivative of sin(x) / x² (when x ≠ 0) is:

$$\frac{\cos(x)x^2 - \sin(x)2x}{x^4}$$

Another example is:

$$f(x) = \frac{2x^2}{x^3}$$

whereas g(x) = 2x² and h(x) = x³, and g'(x) = 4x and h'(x) = 3x².

  a. Differentiation rules
  b. Reciprocal Rule
  c. Constant factor rule in differentiation
  d. Quotient Rule

6. In a totally ordered set all elements are mutually comparable, so such a set can have at most one minimal element and at most one maximal element. Then, due to mutual comparability, the minimal element will also be the least element and the maximal element will also be the greatest element. Thus in a totally ordered set we can simply use the terms minimum and _____.

   a. Nth term
   b. Leibniz rule
   c. Racetrack principle
   d. Maximum

7. In calculus, the _____ is a formula for the derivative of the composite of two functions.

In intuitive terms, if a variable, y, depends on a second variable, u, which in turn depends on a third variable, x, then the rate of change of y with respect to x can be computed as the rate of change of y with respect to u multiplied by the rate of change of u with respect to x. Schematically,

$$\frac{dy}{dx} = \frac{dy}{du} \cdot \frac{du}{dx}.$$

   a. Reciprocal Rule
   b. Product rule
   c. Differentiation rules
   d. Chain Rule

8. In mathematics, a _____ represents the application of one function to the results of another. For instance, the functions f: X → Y and g: Y → Z can be composed by first computing f(x) and then applying a function g to the output of f(x.)

Thus one obtains a function g ∘ f: X → Z defined by (g ∘ f)(x) = g(f(x)) for all x in X. The notation g ∘ f is read as 'g circle f', or 'g composed with f', 'g after f', 'g following f', or just 'g of f'.

   a. Composite function
   b. Piecewise-defined function
   c. Constant function
   d. Surjective

9. A _____ officer is an officer of high military rank. The term or equivalent is used by nearly every country in the world. _____ can be used as a generic term for all grades of _____ officer, or it can specifically refer to a single rank that is just called _____.

Chapter 3. Differentiation

a. BDDC
b. 15 theorem
c. General
d. BIBO stability

10. In mathematics, the simplest case of _____ refers to the study of problems in which one seeks to minimize or maximize a real function by systematically choosing the values of real or integer variables from within an allowed set. This (a scalar real valued objective function) is actually a small subset of this field which comprises a large area of applied mathematics and generalizes to study of means to obtain 'best available' values of some objective function given a defined domain where the elaboration is on the types of functions and the conditions and nature of the objects in the problem domain.

The first _____ technique, which is known as steepest descent, goes back to Gauss.

a. Optimization
b. ACTRAN
c. AUSM
d. ALGOR

11. In economics, _____ is equal to total cost divided by the number of goods produced (the output quantity, Q.) It is also equal to the sum of average variable costs (total variable costs divided by Q) plus average fixed costs (total fixed costs divided by Q.) Average costs may be dependent on the time period considered (increasing production may be expensive or impossible in the short term, for example.)

a. ACTRAN
b. AUSM
c. ALGOR
d. Average cost

12. A _____ is an algebraic equation in which each term is either a constant or the product of a constant and (the first power of) a single variable. Linear equations can have one, two, three or more variables. Linear equations occur with great regularity in applied mathematics.

a. Quadratic formula
b. Cubic function
c. Linear equation
d. Quartic function

13. In mathematics, the _____ of a power series is a non-negative quantity, either a real number or ∞, that represents a domain (within the radius) in which the series will converge. Within the _____, a power series converges absolutely and uniformly on compacta as well. If the series converges, it is the Taylor series of the analytic function to which it converges inside its _____.
   a. Blaschke product
   b. Branch point
   c. Holomorphically separable
   d. Radius of convergence

14. In mathematics, a (topological) _____ is defined as follows: let I be an interval of real numbers (i.e. a non-empty connected subset of $\mathbb{R}$); then a _____ γ is a continuous mapping $\gamma : I \to X$, where X is a topological space. The _____ γ is said to be simple if it is injective, i.e. if for all x, y in I, we have $\gamma(x) = \gamma(y) \implies x = y$. If I is a closed bounded interval $[a, b]$, we also allow the possibility $\gamma(a) = \gamma(b)$ (this convention makes it possible to talk about closed simple _____.)
   a. Tractrix
   b. Closed curve
   c. Prolate cycloid
   d. Curve

15. A _____ is a statement of the meaning of a word or phrase. The term to be defined is known as the definiendum. The words which define it are known as the definiens.
   a. Definition
   b. BDDC
   c. 15 theorem
   d. BIBO stability

16. Let f be a differentiable function, and let f'(x) be its derivative. The derivative of f'(x) (if it has one) is written f''(x) and is called the _____ of f. Similarly, the derivative of a _____, if it exists, is written f'''(x) and is called the third derivative of f.
   a. Vertical asymptote
   b. Slant asymptote
   c. Stationary phase approximation
   d. Second Derivative

Chapter 3. Differentiation

17. In mathematics, the _____ (or replacement set) of a given function is the set of 'input' values for which the function is defined. For instance, the _____ of cosine would be all real numbers, while the _____ of the square root would be only numbers greater than or equal to 0 (ignoring complex numbers in both cases.) In a representation of a function in a xy Cartesian coordinate system, the _____ is represented on the x axis (or abscissa.)

   a. 15 theorem
   b. Domain
   c. BIBO stability
   d. BDDC

18. In calculus, a method called _____ can be applied to implicitly defined functions. This method is an application of the chain rule allowing one to calculate the derivative of a function given implicitly.

As explained in the introduction, y can be given as a function of x implicitly rather than explicitly. When we have an equation R (x,y) = 0, we may be able to solve it for y and then differentiate. However, sometimes it is simpler to differentiate R(x,y) with respect to x and then solve for dy / dx.

   a. Implicit differentiation
   b. Automatic differentiation
   c. Implicit function
   d. Ordinary differential equation

19. In calculus, an _____ is the limit of a definite integral as an endpoint of the interval of integration approaches either a specified real number or ∞ or −∞ or, in some cases, as both endpoints approach limits.

Specifically, an _____ is a limit of the form

$$\lim_{b \to \infty} \int_a^b f(x)\,dx, \qquad \lim_{a \to -\infty} \int_a^b f(x)\,dx,$$

or of the form

$$\lim_{c \to b^-} \int_a^c f(x)\,dx, \qquad \lim_{c \to a^+} \int_c^b f(x)\,dx,$$

in which one takes a limit in one or the other (or sometimes both) endpoints . Improper integrals may also occur at an interior point of the domain of integration, or at multiple such points.

a. Improper integral
b. ALGOR
c. AUSM
d. ACTRAN

20. In mathematics, an _____ is a generalization for the concept of a function in which the dependent variable has not been given 'explicitly' in terms of the independent variable. To give a function f explicitly is to provide a prescription for determining the output value of the function y in terms of the input value x:

y = f(x.)

By contrast, the function is implicit if the value of y is obtained from x by solving an equation of the form:

R(x,y) = 0.

a. Automatic differentiation
b. Implicit function
c. Implicit differentiation
d. Ordinary differential equation

21. Integration is an important concept in mathematics, specifically in the field of calculus and, more broadly, mathematical analysis. Given a function f of a real variable x and an interval [a, b] of the real line, the _____

$$\int_a^b f(x)\,dx,$$

is defined informally to be the net signed area of the region in the xy-plane bounded by the graph of f, the x-axis, and the vertical lines x = a and x = b.

The term '_____' may also refer to the notion of antiderivative, a function F whose derivative is the given function f.

a. Indefinite integral
b. Integral test for convergence
c. Integrand
d. Integral

22.

Chapter 3. Differentiation

In differential calculus, _____ problems involve finding a rate that a quantity changes by relating the population of the earth. The rate of change is usually with respect to people who have died.

a. Standard part function
b. Mean Value Theorem
c. Visual Calculus
d. Related rates

23. In infinitesimal calculus, a _____ is traditionally an infinitesimally small change in a variable. For example, if x is a variable, then a change in the value of x is often denoted Δx (or δx when this change is considered to be small.) The _____ dx represents such a change, but is infinitely small.
   a. The Method of Mechanical Theorems
   b. Dirichlet integral
   c. Local maximum
   d. Differential

Chapter 4. Applications of the Derivative

1. In mathematics, a _____ is a function which preserves the given order. This concept first arose in calculus, and was later generalized to the more abstract setting of order theory.

In calculus, a function f defined on a subset of the real numbers with real values is called monotonic (also monotonically increasing or non-decreasing), if for all x and y such that x >≤ y one has f(x) >≤ f(y), so f preserves the order.

   a. Pettis integral
   b. Pseudo-differential operator
   c. 15 theorem
   d. Monotonic function

2. In a totally ordered set all elements are mutually comparable, so such a set can have at most one minimal element and at most one maximal element. Then, due to mutual comparability, the minimal element will also be the least element and the maximal element will also be the greatest element. Thus in a totally ordered set we can simply use the terms minimum and _____.

   a. Maximum
   b. Leibniz rule
   c. Nth term
   d. Racetrack principle

3. The _____ are a pair of first order, non-linear, differential equations frequently used to describe the dynamics of biological systems in which two species interact, one a predator and one its prey. They were proposed independently by Alfred J. Lotka in 1925 and Vito Volterra in 1926.

   [×] >

   [×] >

where

   - y is the number of some predator;
   - x is the number of its prey;
   - dy/dt and dx/dt represents the growth of the two populations against time;
   - t represents the time; and
   - >α, >β, >γ and >δ are parameters representing the interaction of the two species.

Chapter 4. Applications of the Derivative

When multiplied out, the equations take a form useful for physical interpretation. Their origin should be considered from a more general framework,

$$\frac{dx}{dt} >$$
$$\frac{dy}{dt} >$$

where both functions represent per capita growth rates of the prey and predator, respectively.

a. 15 theorem
b. BDDC
c. BIBO stability
d. Lotka-Volterra equations

4. The _____ of a material is defined as its mass per unit volume. The symbol of _____ is ρ '>rho.)

Mathematically:

$$d = \frac{m}{V}$$

where:

    d is the _____,
    m is the mass,
    V is the volume.

a. 15 theorem
b. BDDC
c. BIBO stability
d. Density

5. In mathematics, a probability _____ is a function that represents a probability distribution in terms of integrals.

Chapter 4. Applications of the Derivative

Formally, a probability distribution has density f, if f is a non-negative Lebesgue-integrable function $\mathbb{R} \to \mathbb{R}$ such that the probability of the interval [a, b] is given by

$$\int_a^b f(x)\,dx$$

for any two numbers a and b. This implies that the total integral of f must be 1.

a. 15 theorem
b. Density function
c. Factorial moment generating function
d. BDDC

6. In a totally ordered set all elements are mutually comparable, so such a set can have at most one minimal element and at most one maximal element. Then, due to mutual comparability, the minimal element will also be the least element and the maximal element will also be the greatest element. Thus in a totally ordered set we can simply use the terms _____ and maximum.

a. Maximum
b. Minimum
c. Ghosts of departed quantities
d. Nth term

7. _____ is a way of expressing knowledge or belief that an event will occur or has occurred. In mathematics the concept has been given an exact meaning in _____ theory, that is used extensively in such areas of study as mathematics, statistics, finance, gambling, science, and philosophy to draw conclusions about the likelihood of potential events and the underlying mechanics of complex systems.

The word _____ does not have a consistent direct definition.

a. Linear regression
b. Discrete probability distributions
c. Normal distribution
d. Probability.

8. In mathematics, a _____ (pdf) is a function that represents a probability distribution in terms of integrals.

Chapter 4. Applications of the Derivative 33

Formally, a probability distribution has density f, if f is a non-negative Lebesgue-integrable function $\mathbb{R} \to \mathbb{R}$ such that the probability of the interval [a, b] is given by

$$\int_a^b f(x)\, dx$$

for any two numbers a and b. This implies that the total integral of f must be 1.

    a. Probability density function
    b. Factorial moment generating function
    c. BDDC
    d. 15 theorem

9. In mathematics, a _____ (or critical number) is a point on the domain of a function where:

- one dimension: the derivative (or slope of the line when visualized) is equal to zero or a point where the function ceases to be differentiable.
- in general: there are two distinct concepts: either the derivative (Jacobian) vanishes, or it is not of full rank (or, in either case, the function is not differentiable); these agree in one dimension.

Note that in one dimension, a critical value or critical number x of function f is the domain element at which the derivative is zero or undefined, whereas the associated ordered pair (x, y) is the _____. In higher dimensions a critical value is in the range whereas a _____ is in the domain.

There are two situations in which a point becomes a _____ of a function of one variable. The first of which is that the value of the first derivative is equal to zero.

    a. Total derivative
    b. Differentiation operator
    c. Critical point
    d. Multivariable calculus

10. In calculus, a branch of mathematics, the _____ is a measurement of how a function changes when its input changes. Loosely speaking, a _____ can be thought of as how much a quantity is changing at some given point. For example, the _____ of the position (or distance) of a vehicle with respect to time is the instantaneous velocity (respectively, instantaneous speed) at which the vehicle is traveling.

The process of finding a _____ is called differentiation. The fundamental theorem of calculus states that differentiation is the reverse process to integration.

a. Derivative
b. Semi-differentiability
c. Bounded function
d. Stationary phase approximation

11. In calculus, the _____ determines whether a given critical point of a function is a maximum, a minimum, or neither.

Suppose that f is a function and we want to determine if f has a maximum or minimum at x. If f is increasing to the left of x and decreasing to the right of x, then x is a local maximum of f.

a. Test for Divergence
b. Continuous function
c. First Derivative Test
d. Partial sum

12. In differential calculus, an inflection point, or _____ (or inflexion) is a point on a curve at which the curvature changes sign. The curve changes from being concave upwards (positive curvature) to concave downwards (negative curvature), or vice versa. If one imagines driving a vehicle along the curve, it is a point at which the steering-wheel is momentarily 'straight', being turned from left to right or vice versa.

a. Derivative of a constant
b. Logarithmic derivative
c. Lin-Tsien equation
d. Point of inflection

13. Let f be a differentiable function, and let f'(x) be its derivative. The derivative of f'(x) (if it has one) is written f''(x) and is called the _____ of f. Similarly, the derivative of a _____, if it exists, is written f'''(x) and is called the third derivative of f.

a. Second Derivative
b. Vertical asymptote
c. Slant asymptote
d. Stationary phase approximation

14. In calculus, a branch of mathematics, the _____ is a criterion often useful for determining whether a given stationary point of a function is a local maximum or a local minimum.

Chapter 4. Applications of the Derivative

The test states: If the function f is twice differentiable at a stationary point x, meaning that $f'(x) = 0$, then:

- If $f''(x) < 0$ then f has a local maximum at x.
- If $f''(x) > 0$ then f has a local minimum at x.
- If $f''(x) = 0$, the _____ says nothing about the point x, has a possible inflection point.

In the last case, the function may have a local maximum or minimum there, but the function is sufficiently 'flat' that this is undetected by the second derivative. In this case one has to examine the third derivative. Such an example is f(x) = x⁴.

a. Symmetric derivative
b. Second Derivative Test
c. Stationary point
d. Linearity of differentiation

15. An _____ of a real-valued function y = f(x) is a curve which describes the behavior of f as either x or y tends to infinity.

In other words, as one moves along the graph of f(x) in some direction, the distance between it and the _____ eventually becomes smaller than any distance that one may specify.

a. AUSM
b. ALGOR
c. ACTRAN
d. Asymptote

16. The line x = a is a _____ of a curve y=f(x) if at least one of the following statements is true:

1. $\lim_{x \to a} f(x) = \pm\infty$
2. $\lim_{x \to a^-} f(x) = \pm\infty$
3. $\lim_{x \to a^+} f(x) = \pm\infty$

Intuitively, if x = a is an asymptote of f, then, if we imagine x approaching a from one side, the value of f(x) grows without bound; i.e., f(x) becomes large (positively or negatively), and, in fact, becomes larger than any finite value.

Chapter 4. Applications of the Derivative

Note that f(x) may or may not be defined at a: what the function is doing precisely at x = a does not affect the asymptote. For example, consider the function

$$f(x) = \begin{cases} \frac{1}{x} & \text{if } x > 0, \\ 5 & \text{if } x \leq 0 \end{cases}$$

As $x \to 0^+$, $\lim_{x \to 0^+} f(x) = \infty$, f(x) has a _____ at 0, even though f(0) = 5.

Another example is $f(x) = 1/(x-1)$ which has a _____ of x=1 as shown by the limit

$$\lim_{x \to 1^+} \frac{1}{x-1} = \infty$$

In the graph of $f(x) = x + \frac{1}{x}$, the y-axis (x = 0) and the line y = x are both asymptotes.

When a linear asymptote is not parallel to the x- or y-axis, it is called either an oblique asymptote or equivalently a slant asymptote.

a. Third derivative
b. Monodromy
c. Ramp function
d. Vertical asymptote

17. Suppose f is a function. Then the line y = a is a _____ for f if

$$\lim_{x \to \infty} f(x) = a \text{ or } \lim_{x \to -\infty} f(x) = a.$$

Intuitively, this means that f(x) can be made as close as desired to a by making x big enough. How big is big enough depends on how close one wishes to make f(x) to a.

a. Second derivative
b. Horizontal asymptote
c. Mountain pass theorem
d. Third derivative

Chapter 4. Applications of the Derivative

18. In mathematics, a (topological) _____ is defined as follows: let I be an interval of real numbers (i.e. a non-empty connected subset of $\mathbb{R}$); then a _____ γ is a continuous mapping $\gamma : I \to X$, where X is a topological space. The _____ γ is said to be simple if it is injective, i.e. if for all x, y in I, we have $\gamma(x) = \gamma(y) \implies x = y$. If I is a closed bounded interval $[a, b]$, we also allow the possibility $\gamma(a) = \gamma(b)$ (this convention makes it possible to talk about closed simple _____.)

   a. Closed curve
   b. Prolate cycloid
   c. Tractrix
   d. Curve

19. In mathematics, the simplest case of _____ refers to the study of problems in which one seeks to minimize or maximize a real function by systematically choosing the values of real or integer variables from within an allowed set. This (a scalar real valued objective function) is actually a small subset of this field which comprises a large area of applied mathematics and generalizes to study of means to obtain 'best available' values of some objective function given a defined domain where the elaboration is on the types of functions and the conditions and nature of the objects in the problem domain.

   The first _____ technique, which is known as steepest descent, goes back to Gauss.

   a. AUSM
   b. ACTRAN
   c. Optimization
   d. ALGOR

20. The largest and the smallest element of a set are called extreme values, absolute extrema, or extreme records.

   For a differentiable function f, if $f(x_0)$ is an _____ for the set of all values f(x), and if x_0 is in the interior of the domain of f, then x_0 is a critical point, by Fermat's theorem.

   In the case of a general partial order one should not confuse a least element (smaller than all other) and a minimal element (nothing is smaller.)

   a. Integration by substitution
   b. Extreme Value Theorem
   c. Infinitesimal
   d. Extreme value

21. Integration is an important concept in mathematics, specifically in the field of calculus and, more broadly, mathematical analysis. Given a function f of a real variable x and an interval [a, b] of the real line, the _____

$$\int_a^b f(x)\,dx,$$

is defined informally to be the net signed area of the region in the xy-plane bounded by the graph of f, the x-axis, and the vertical lines x = a and x = b.

The term '_____' may also refer to the notion of antiderivative, a function F whose derivative is the given function f.

a. Integrand
b. Indefinite integral
c. Integral test for convergence
d. Integral

Chapter 5. Exponential and Logarithmic Functions

1. The _____ is a function in mathematics. The application of this function to a value x is written as exp(x). Equivalently, this can be written in the form e^x, where e is a mathematical constant, the base of the natural logarithm, which equals approximately 2.718281828, and is also known as Euler's number.

   a. Exponential function
   b. ACTRAN
   c. Integral part
   d. Area hyperbolic functions

2. In calculus, an _____ is the limit of a definite integral as an endpoint of the interval of integration approaches either a specified real number or ∞ or −∞ or, in some cases, as both endpoints approach limits.

Specifically, an _____ is a limit of the form

$$\lim_{b\to\infty} \int_a^b f(x)\,dx, \qquad \lim_{a\to-\infty} \int_a^b f(x)\,dx,$$

or of the form

$$\lim_{c\to b^-} \int_a^c f(x)\,dx, \qquad \lim_{c\to a^+} \int_c^b f(x)\,dx,$$

in which one takes a limit in one or the other (or sometimes both) endpoints . Improper integrals may also occur at an interior point of the domain of integration, or at multiple such points.

   a. ACTRAN
   b. Improper integral
   c. AUSM
   d. ALGOR

3. Integration is an important concept in mathematics, specifically in the field of calculus and, more broadly, mathematical analysis. Given a function f of a real variable x and an interval [a, b] of the real line, the _____

$$\int_a^b f(x)\,dx,$$

is defined informally to be the net signed area of the region in the xy-plane bounded by the graph of f, the x-axis, and the vertical lines x = a and x = b.

The term '_____' may also refer to the notion of antiderivative, a function F whose derivative is the given function f.

a. Indefinite integral
b. Integral test for convergence
c. Integral
d. Integrand

4. This article will state and prove the _____ for differentiation, and then use it to prove these two formulas.

The _____ for differentiation states that for every natural number n, the derivative of $f(x) = x^n$ is $f'(x) = nx^{n-1}$, that is,

$$(x^n)' = nx^{n-1}.$$

The _____ for integration

$$\int x^n \, dx = \frac{x^{n+1}}{n+1} + C$$

for natural n is then an easy consequence. One just needs to take the derivative of this equality and use the _____ and linearity of differentiation on the right-hand side.

a. Functional integration
b. Power Rule
c. Test for Divergence
d. Leibniz rule

5. The natural logarithm, formerly known as the hyperbolic logarithm, is the logarithm to the _____, where e is an irrational constant approximately equal to 2.718281828. It is also sometimes referred to as the Napierian logarithm, although the original meaning of this term is slightly different. In simple terms, the natural logarithm of a number x is the power to which e would have to be raised to equal x -- for example the natural log of e itself is 1 because e^1 = e, while the natural logarithm of 1 would be 0, since e^0 = 1.
a. BDDC
b. BIBO stability
c. 15 theorem
d. Base e

Chapter 5. Exponential and Logarithmic Functions

6. The _____, formerly known as the hyperbolic logarithm, is the logarithm to the base e, where e is an irrational constant approximately equal to 2.718281828. It is also sometimes referred to as the Napierian logarithm, although the original meaning of this term is slightly different. In simple terms, the _____ of a number x is the power to which e would have to be raised to equal x -- for example the natural log of e itself is 1 because e^1 = e, while the _____ of 1 would be 0, since e^0 = 1.
   a. 15 theorem
   b. Natural logarithm
   c. BIBO stability
   d. BDDC

7. Just as the definite integral of a positive function of one variable represents the area of the region between the graph of the function and the x-axis, the _____ of a positive function of two variables represents the volume of the region between the surface defined by the function (on the three dimensional Cartesian plane where z = f(x,y)) and the plane which contains its domain. (Note that the same volume can be obtained via the triple integral -- the integral of a function in three variables -- of the constant function f(x, y, z) = 1 over the above-mentioned region between the surface and the plane.) If there are more variables, a multiple integral will yield hypervolumes of multi-dimensional functions.
   a. Trigonometric substitution
   b. Risch algorithm
   c. Constant of integration
   d. Double integral

8. The function $\log_b(x)$ depends on both b and x, but the term _____ in standard usage refers to a function of the form $\log_b(x)$ in which the base b is fixed and so the only argument is x. Thus there is one _____ for each value of the base b (which must be positive and must differ from 1.) Viewed in this way, the base-b _____ is the inverse function of the exponential function b^x.
   a. BDDC
   b. 15 theorem
   c. BIBO stability
   d. Logarithm function

9. In mathematics, the _____ of a function y = f(x) is a function that, in some fashion, 'undoes' the effect of f The _____ of f is denoted f^{-1}. The statements y=f(x) and x=f^{-1}(y) are equivalent.
   a. ALGOR
   b. ACTRAN
   c. AUSM
   d. Inverse

Chapter 5. Exponential and Logarithmic Functions

10. In mathematics, if f is a function from A to B then an _____ for f is a function in the opposite direction, from B to A, with the property that a round trip (a composition) from A to B to A (or from B to A to B) returns each element of the initial set to itself. Thus, if an input x into the function f produces an output y, then inputting y into the _____ f^{-1} (read f inverse, not to be confused with exponentiation) produces the output x. Not every function has an inverse; those that do are called invertible.
    a. Augustin Louis Cauchy
    b. Aristotle
    c. Augustin-Jean Fresnel
    d. Inverse function

11. _____ is the concept of adding accumulated interest back to the principal, so that interest is earned on interest from that moment on. The act of declaring interest to be principal is called compounding (i.e., interest is compounded.) A loan, for example, may have its interest compounded every month: in this case, a loan with $100 principal and 1% interest per month would have a balance of $101 at the end of the first month.
    a. 15 theorem
    b. BDDC
    c. BIBO stability
    d. Compound interest

12. In mathematics, a (topological) _____ is defined as follows: let I be an interval of real numbers (i.e. a non-empty connected subset of $\mathbb{R}$); then a _____ γ is a continuous mapping $\gamma : I \to X$, where X is a topological space. The _____ γ is said to be simple if it is injective, i.e. if for all x, y in I, we have $\gamma(x) = \gamma(y) \implies x = y$. If I is a closed bounded interval $[a, b]$, we also allow the possibility $\gamma(a) = \gamma(b)$ (this convention makes it possible to talk about closed simple _____.)
    a. Tractrix
    b. Curve
    c. Prolate cycloid
    d. Closed curve

13. In mathematics, the _____ is a conic section, the intersection of a right circular conical surface and a plane parallel to a generating straight line of that surface. Given a point (the focus) and a line (the directrix) that lie in a plane, the locus of points in that plane that are equidistant to them is a _____.

A particular case arises when the plane is tangent to the conical surface of a circle.

Chapter 5. Exponential and Logarithmic Functions

a. BIBO stability
b. Parabola
c. 15 theorem
d. BDDC

14. In mathematics, a _____ of a function of several variables is its derivative with respect to one of those variables with the others held constant (as opposed to the total derivative, in which all variables are allowed to vary.) Partial derivatives are useful in vector calculus and differential geometry.

The _____ of a function f with respect to the variable x is written as f'_x, $\partial_x f$, or $\partial f/\partial x$.

a. Jacobian
b. Differentiation operator
c. Level curve
d. Partial derivative

15. In calculus, a branch of mathematics, the _____ is a measurement of how a function changes when its input changes. Loosely speaking, a _____ can be thought of as how much a quantity is changing at some given point. For example, the _____ of the position (or distance) of a vehicle with respect to time is the instantaneous velocity (respectively, instantaneous speed) at which the vehicle is traveling.

The process of finding a _____ is called differentiation. The fundamental theorem of calculus states that differentiation is the reverse process to integration.

a. Bounded function
b. Stationary phase approximation
c. Semi-differentiability
d. Derivative

16. In a totally ordered set all elements are mutually comparable, so such a set can have at most one minimal element and at most one maximal element. Then, due to mutual comparability, the minimal element will also be the least element and the maximal element will also be the greatest element. Thus in a totally ordered set we can simply use the terms minimum and _____.

a. Maximum
b. Nth term
c. Racetrack principle
d. Leibniz rule

17. In calculus, the _____ is a formula for the derivative of the composite of two functions.

In intuitive terms, if a variable, y, depends on a second variable, u, which in turn depends on a third variable, x, then the rate of change of y with respect to x can be computed as the rate of change of y with respect to u multiplied by the rate of change of u with respect to x. Schematically,

$$\frac{dy}{dx} = \frac{dy}{du} \cdot \frac{du}{dx}.$$

a. Reciprocal Rule
b. Product rule
c. Differentiation rules
d. Chain Rule

18. In mathematics, specifically in calculus and complex analysis, the _____ of a function f is defined by the formula

$$\frac{f'}{f}$$

where f ' is the derivative of f.

When f is a function f(x) of a real variable x, and takes real, strictly positive values, this is indeed the formula for (log f)', that is, the derivative of the natural logarithm of f, as follows directly from the chain rule.

Many properties of the real logarithm also apply to the _____, even when the function does not take values in the positive reals.

a. Lin-Tsien equation
b. Point of inflection
c. Directional derivative
d. Logarithmic derivative

19. _____ (including exponential decay) occurs when the growth rate of a mathematical function is proportional to the function's current value. In the case of a discrete domain of definition with equal intervals it is also called geometric growth or geometric decay (the function values form a geometric progression.)

_____ is said to follow an exponential law; the simple-_____ model is known as the Malthusian growth model.

Chapter 5. Exponential and Logarithmic Functions

a. Isomonodromic deformation
b. Oscillating
c. Inseparable differential equation
d. Exponential growth

20. _____ is a type of motion in which the velocity of an object changes equal amounts in equal time periods. An example of an object having _____ would be a ball rolling down a ramp. The object picks up velocity as it goes down the ramp with equal changes in time.
   a. Uniform Acceleration
   b. AUSM
   c. ACTRAN
   d. ALGOR

21. A quantity is said to be subject to _____ if it decreases at a rate proportional to its value. Symbolically, this can be expressed as the following differential equation, where N is the quantity and λ is a positive number called the decay constant.

$$\frac{dN}{dt} = -\lambda N.$$

The solution to this equation is:

$$N(t) = N_0 e^{-\lambda t}.$$

Here N(t) is the quantity at time t, and N_0 = N(0) is the initial quantity, i.e. the quantity at time t = 0.

   a. ALGOR
   b. Exponential decay
   c. ACTRAN
   d. Exponential sum

22. The _____ of a quantity whose value decreases with time is the interval required for the quantity to decay to half of its initial value. The concept originated in describing how long it takes atoms to undergo radioactive decay but also applies in a wide variety of other situations.

The term '_____' dates to 1907.

a. BDDC
b. BIBO stability
c. 15 theorem
d. Half-life

23. A _____ in biology generally concerns a measured property such as population size, body height or biomass. Values for the measured property can be plotted on a graph as a function of time.
a. Spectral theory of ordinary differential equations
b. Variation of parameters
c. Cauchy-Euler equation
d. Growth curve

Chapter 6. Integration

1. In calculus, an _____, primitive or indefinite integral of a function f is a function F whose derivative is equal to f, i.e., F >' = f. The process of solving for antiderivatives is antidifferentiation (or indefinite integration.) Antiderivatives are related to definite integrals through the fundamental theorem of calculus: the definite integral of a function over an interval is equal to the difference between the values of an _____ evaluated at the endpoints of the interval.
    a. Order of integration
    b. Integrand
    c. Indefinite integral
    d. Antiderivative

2. _____ is a type of motion in which the velocity of an object changes equal amounts in equal time periods. An example of an object having _____ would be a ball rolling down a ramp. The object picks up velocity as it goes down the ramp with equal changes in time.
    a. Uniform Acceleration
    b. ACTRAN
    c. ALGOR
    d. AUSM

3. In calculus, the indefinite integral of a given function (i.e. the set of all antiderivatives of the function) is always written with a constant, the _____. This constant expresses an ambiguity inherent in the construction of antiderivatives. If a function f(x) is defined on an interval and F(x) is an antiderivative of f(x), then the set of all antiderivatives of f(x) is given by the functions F(x) + C, where C is an arbitrary constant.
    a. Nonelementary integral
    b. Constant of integration
    c. Disk integration
    d. Sum rule in integration

4. The _____ is a function in mathematics. The application of this function to a value x is written as exp(x). Equivalently, this can be written in the form e^x, where e is a mathematical constant, the base of the natural logarithm, which equals approximately 2.718281828, and is also known as Euler's number.
    a. Exponential function
    b. Integral part
    c. ACTRAN
    d. Area hyperbolic functions

5. In calculus, an antiderivative, primitive or _____ of a function f is a function F whose derivative is equal to f, i.e., F ' = f. The process of solving for antiderivatives is antidifferentiation (or indefinite integration.) Antiderivatives are related to definite integrals through the fundamental theorem of calculus: the definite integral of a function over an interval is equal to the difference between the values of an antiderivative evaluated at the endpoints of the interval.

a. Integral test for convergence
b. Arc length
c. Integration by parts operator
d. Indefinite integral

6. If a function has an integral, it is said to be integrable. The function for which the integral is calculated is called the _____. The region over which a function is being integrated is called the domain of integration.
   a. Integrand
   b. Order of integration
   c. Integral test for convergence
   d. Integration by parts

7. Integration is an important concept in mathematics, specifically in the field of calculus and, more broadly, mathematical analysis. Given a function f of a real variable x and an interval [a, b] of the real line, the _____

$$\int_a^b f(x)\,dx,$$

is defined informally to be the net signed area of the region in the xy-plane bounded by the graph of f, the x-axis, and the vertical lines x = a and x = b.

The term '_____' may also refer to the notion of antiderivative, a function F whose derivative is the given function f.

   a. Integral
   b. Indefinite integral
   c. Integrand
   d. Integral test for convergence

8. Just as the definite integral of a positive function of one variable represents the area of the region between the graph of the function and the x-axis, the _____ of a positive function of two variables represents the volume of the region between the surface defined by the function (on the three dimensional Cartesian plane where z = f(x,y)) and the plane which contains its domain. (Note that the same volume can be obtained via the triple integral -- the integral of a function in three variables -- of the constant function f(x, y, z) = 1 over the above-mentioned region between the surface and the plane.) If there are more variables, a multiple integral will yield hypervolumes of multi-dimensional functions.

a. Constant of integration
b. Trigonometric substitution
c. Risch algorithm
d. Double integral

9. A quantity is said to be subject to _____ if it decreases at a rate proportional to its value. Symbolically, this can be expressed as the following differential equation, where N is the quantity and λ is a positive number called the decay constant.

$$\frac{dN}{dt} = -\lambda N.$$

The solution to this equation is:

$$N(t) = N_0 e^{-\lambda t}.$$

Here N(t) is the quantity at time t, and N_0 = N(0) is the initial quantity, i.e. the quantity at time t = 0.

a. Exponential sum
b. ACTRAN
c. ALGOR
d. Exponential decay

10. In mathematics, _____ and minima, known collectively as extrema, are the largest value (maximum) or smallest value (minimum), that a function takes in a point either within a given neighbourhood (local extremum) or on the function domain in its entirety (global extremum.)

Throughout, a point refers to an input (x), while a value refers to an output (y): one distinguishing between the maximum value and the point (or points) at which it occurs.

A real-valued function f defined on the real line is said to have a local maximum point at the point x*, if there exists some ε > 0, such that f(x*) ≥ f(x) when |x − x*| < ε.

a. Maxima
b. Leibniz formula
c. Related rates
d. Racetrack principle

11. In calculus, a _____ is either of the two limits of a function f(x) of a real variable x as x approaches a specified point either from below or from above. One should write either:

$$\lim_{x \to a^+} f(x) \text{ or } \lim_{x \downarrow a} f(x)$$

for the limit as x decreases in value approaching a (x approaches a 'from above' or 'from the right'), and similarly

$$\lim_{x \to a^-} f(x) \text{ or } \lim_{x \uparrow a} f(x)$$

for the limit as x increases in value approaching a (x approaches a 'from below' or 'from the left'.)

The two one-sided limits exist and are equal if and only if the limit of f(x) as x approaches a exists.

a. ALGOR
b. AUSM
c. ACTRAN
d. One-sided limit

12. In mathematics, the simplest case of _____ refers to the study of problems in which one seeks to minimize or maximize a real function by systematically choosing the values of real or integer variables from within an allowed set. This (a scalar real valued objective function) is actually a small subset of this field which comprises a large area of applied mathematics and generalizes to study of means to obtain 'best available' values of some objective function given a defined domain where the elaboration is on the types of functions and the conditions and nature of the objects in the problem domain.

The first _____ technique, which is known as steepest descent, goes back to Gauss.

a. ALGOR
b. AUSM
c. ACTRAN
d. Optimization

13. This article will state and prove the _____ for differentiation, and then use it to prove these two formulas.

Chapter 6. Integration

The _____ for differentiation states that for every natural number n, the derivative of $f(x) = x^n$ is $f'(x) = nx^{n-1}$, that is,

$$(x^n)' = nx^{n-1}.$$

The _____ for integration

$$\int x^n \, dx = \frac{x^{n+1}}{n+1} + C$$

for natural n is then an easy consequence. One just needs to take the derivative of this equality and use the _____ and linearity of differentiation on the right-hand side.

a. Test for Divergence
b. Power Rule
c. Leibniz rule
d. Functional integration

14. In mathematics, the concept of a '_____' is used to describe the behavior of a function as its argument or input either 'gets close' to some point, or as the argument becomes arbitrarily large; or the behavior of a sequence's elements as their index increases indefinitely. Limits are used in calculus and other branches of mathematical analysis to define derivatives and continuity.

In formulas, _____ is usually abbreviated as lim

a. BIBO stability
b. Limit
c. 15 theorem
d. BDDC

15. The _____ of a material is defined as its mass per unit volume. The symbol of _____ is ρ '>rho.)

Mathematically:

$$d = \frac{m}{V}$$

where:

> d is the _____,
> m is the mass,
> V is the volume.

a. BIBO stability
b. BDDC
c. Density
d. 15 theorem

16. In mathematics, a probability _____ is a function that represents a probability distribution in terms of integrals.

Formally, a probability distribution has density f, if f is a non-negative Lebesgue-integrable function $\mathbb{R} \to \mathbb{R}$ such that the probability of the interval [a, b] is given by

$$\int_a^b f(x)\,dx$$

for any two numbers a and b. This implies that the total integral of f must be 1.

a. Factorial moment generating function
b. 15 theorem
c. BDDC
d. Density function

17. In calculus, a branch of mathematics, the _____ is a measurement of how a function changes when its input changes. Loosely speaking, a _____ can be thought of as how much a quantity is changing at some given point. For example, the _____ of the position (or distance) of a vehicle with respect to time is the instantaneous velocity (respectively, instantaneous speed) at which the vehicle is traveling.

The process of finding a _____ is called differentiation. The fundamental theorem of calculus states that differentiation is the reverse process to integration.

a. Semi-differentiability
b. Derivative
c. Stationary phase approximation
d. Bounded function

Chapter 6. Integration

18. The function log_b(x) depends on both b and x, but the term _____ in standard usage refers to a function of the form log_b(x) in which the base b is fixed and so the only argument is x. Thus there is one _____ for each value of the base b (which must be positive and must differ from 1.) Viewed in this way, the base-b _____ is the inverse function of the exponential function b^x.

   a. BIBO stability
   b. BDDC
   c. Logarithm function
   d. 15 theorem

19. In mathematics, in the field of differential equations, an _____ is an ordinary differential equation together with specified value, called the initial condition, of the unknown function at a given point in the domain of the solution. In physics or other sciences, modeling a system frequently amounts to solving an _____; in this context, the differential equation is an evolution equation specifying how, given initial conditions, the system will evolve with time.

   An _____ is a differential equation

   $$y'(t) = f(t, y(t)) \quad \text{with} \quad f : \mathbb{R} \times \mathbb{R} \to \mathbb{R}$$

   together with a point in the domain of f

   $$(t_0, y_0) \in \mathbb{R} \times \mathbb{R},$$

   called the initial condition.

   a. Initial value problem
   b. AUSM
   c. ACTRAN
   d. ALGOR

20. In mathematics, a (topological) _____ is defined as follows: let I be an interval of real numbers (i.e. a non-empty connected subset of $\mathbb{R}$); then a _____ γ is a continuous mapping $\gamma : I \to X$, where X is a topological space. The _____ γ is said to be simple if it is injective, i.e. if for all x, y in I, we have $\gamma(x) = \gamma(y) \implies x = y$. If I is a closed bounded interval $[a, b]$, we also allow the possibility $\gamma(a) = \gamma(b)$ (this convention makes it possible to talk about closed simple _____.)

   a. Curve
   b. Closed curve
   c. Tractrix
   d. Prolate cycloid

Chapter 6. Integration

21. In mathematics, a _____ is a method for approximating the total area underneath a curve on a graph, otherwise known as an integral. It may also be used to define the integration operation.

Consider a function $f: D \to \mathbf{R}$, where D is a subset of the real numbers $\mathbf{R}$, and let $I = [a, b]$ be a closed interval contained in D. A finite set of points $\{x_0, x_1, x_2, ... x_n\}$ such that $a = x_0 < x_1 < x_2 ... < x_n = b$ creates a partition

$$P = \{[x_0, x_1), [x_1, x_2), ... [x_{n-1}, x_n]\}$$

of I.

a. Signed measure
b. Solid of revolution
c. Risch algorithm
d. Riemann sum

22. In calculus and mathematical analysis the _____ of the integral

$$\int_a^b f(x)\, dx$$

of a Riemann integrable function f defined on a closed and bounded interval [a, b] are the real numbers a and b.

_____ can also be defined for improper integrals, with the _____ of both

$$\lim_{z \to a+} \int_z^b f(x)\, dx$$

and

$$\lim_{z \to b-} \int_a^z f(x)\, dx$$

again being a and b. For an improper integral

$$\int_a^\infty f(x)\, dx$$

or

$$\int_{-\infty}^{b} f(x)\,dx$$

the _____ are a and ∞, or −∞ and b, respectively.

   a. Test for Divergence
   b. Differential
   c. Maxima
   d. Limits of integration

23. In numerical analysis, _____ constitutes a broad family of algorithms for calculating the numerical value of a definite integral, and by extension, the term is also sometimes used to describe the numerical solution of differential equations The term numerical quadrature is more or less a synonym for _____, especially as applied to one-dimensional integrals.
   a. Meshfree methods
   b. Galerkin methods
   c. Multigrid method
   d. Numerical integration

24. In mathematics, engineering, and manufacturing, a _____ is a solid figure obtained by rotating a plane curve around some straight line (the axis) that lies on the same plane.

Assuming that the curve does not cross the axis, the solid's volume is equal to the length of the circle described by the figure's centroid, times the figure's area (Pappus's second centroid Theorem.)

Rotating a curve

A representative disk is a three-dimensional volume element of a _____.

   a. Surface of revolution
   b. Trigonometric substitution
   c. Riemann sum
   d. Solid of revolution

25. The _____ of any solid, liquid, plasma, vacuum or theoretical object is how much three-dimensional space it occupies, often quantified numerically. One-dimensional figures (such as lines) and two-dimensional shapes (such as squares) are assigned zero _____ in the three-dimensional space. _____ is commonly presented in units such as mL or cm^3 (milliliters or cubic centimeters.)
   a. Klein-Gordon equation
   b. Vector potential
   c. Dirac equation
   d. Volume

Chapter 7. Additional Topics in Integration

1. In mathematics, the _____ is a way to approximately calculate the definite integral

$$\int_a^b f(x)\,dx.$$

The _____ works by approximating the region under the graph of the function f by a trapezoid and calculating its area. It follows that

$$\int_a^b f(x)\,dx \approx (b-a)\frac{f(a)+f(b)}{2}.$$

To calculate this integral more accurately, one first splits the interval of integration [a,b] into n smaller subintervals, and then applies the _____ on each of them. One obtains the composite _____:

$$\int_a^b f(x)\,dx \approx \frac{b-a}{n}\left[\frac{f(a)+f(b)}{2} + \sum_{k=1}^{n-1} f\left(a+k\frac{b-a}{n}\right)\right].$$

This can alternatively be written as:

$$\int_a^b f(x)\,dx \approx \frac{b-a}{2n}\left(f(x_0) + 2f(x_1) + 2f(x_2) + \cdots + 2f(x_{n-1}) + f(x_n)\right)$$

where

$$x_k = a + k\frac{b-a}{n}, \text{ for } k = 0, 1, \ldots, n$$

(one can also use a non-uniform grid.)

 a. BIBO stability
 b. BDDC
 c. 15 theorem
 d. Trapezoidal Rule

2. In numerical analysis, _____ constitutes a broad family of algorithms for calculating the numerical value of a definite integral, and by extension, the term is also sometimes used to describe the numerical solution of differential equations The term numerical quadrature is more or less a synonym for _____, especially as applied to one-dimensional integrals.

Chapter 7. Additional Topics in Integration

a. Meshfree methods
b. Numerical integration
c. Galerkin methods
d. Multigrid method

3. The _____ is a function in mathematics. The application of this function to a value x is written as exp(x). Equivalently, this can be written in the form e^x, where e is a mathematical constant, the base of the natural logarithm, which equals approximately 2.718281828, and is also known as Euler's number.

a. ACTRAN
b. Integral part
c. Area hyperbolic functions
d. Exponential function

4. In calculus, an _____ is the limit of a definite integral as an endpoint of the interval of integration approaches either a specified real number or ∞ or −∞ or, in some cases, as both endpoints approach limits.

Specifically, an _____ is a limit of the form

$$\lim_{b \to \infty} \int_a^b f(x)\,dx, \qquad \lim_{a \to -\infty} \int_a^b f(x)\,dx,$$

or of the form

$$\lim_{c \to b^-} \int_a^c f(x)\,dx, \qquad \lim_{c \to a^+} \int_c^b f(x)\,dx,$$

in which one takes a limit in one or the other (or sometimes both) endpoints . Improper integrals may also occur at an interior point of the domain of integration, or at multiple such points.

a. AUSM
b. ACTRAN
c. ALGOR
d. Improper integral

5. Integration is an important concept in mathematics, specifically in the field of calculus and, more broadly, mathematical analysis. Given a function f of a real variable x and an interval [a, b] of the real line, the _____

$$\int_a^b f(x)\,dx,$$

is defined informally to be the net signed area of the region in the xy-plane bounded by the graph of f, the x-axis, and the vertical lines x = a and x = b.

The term '_____' may also refer to the notion of antiderivative, a function F whose derivative is the given function f.

a. Indefinite integral
b. Integrand
c. Integral
d. Integral test for convergence

Chapter 8. Calculus of Several Variables

1. The _____ of a material is defined as its mass per unit volume. The symbol of _____ is ρ ('>rho.)

Mathematically:

$$d = \frac{m}{V}$$

where:

    d is the _____,
    m is the mass,
    V is the volume.

a. BDDC
b. BIBO stability
c. 15 theorem
d. Density

2. In mathematics, a probability _____ is a function that represents a probability distribution in terms of integrals.

Formally, a probability distribution has density f, if f is a non-negative Lebesgue-integrable function $\mathbb{R} \to \mathbb{R}$ such that the probability of the interval [a, b] is given by

$$\int_a^b f(x)\,dx$$

for any two numbers a and b. This implies that the total integral of f must be 1.

a. 15 theorem
b. BDDC
c. Factorial moment generating function
d. Density function

3. In mathematics, the _____ (or replacement set) of a given function is the set of 'input' values for which the function is defined. For instance, the _____ of cosine would be all real numbers, while the _____ of the square root would be only numbers greater than or equal to 0 (ignoring complex numbers in both cases.) In a representation of a function in a xy Cartesian coordinate system, the _____ is represented on the x axis (or abscissa.)

Chapter 8. Calculus of Several Variables

a. 15 theorem
b. BDDC
c. BIBO stability
d. Domain

4. The terms '_____' and 'independent variable' are used in similar but subtly different ways in mathematics and statistics as part of the standard terminology in those subjects. They are used to distinguish between two types of quantities being considered, separating them into those available at the start of a process and those being created by it, where the latter (dependent variables) are dependent on the former (independent variables.)

In traditional calculus, a function is defined as a relation between two terms called variables because their values vary.

a. 15 theorem
b. Dependent variable
c. BIBO stability
d. BDDC

5. The _____ is a function in mathematics. The application of this function to a value x is written as exp(x). Equivalently, this can be written in the form e^x, where e is a mathematical constant, the base of the natural logarithm, which equals approximately 2.718281828, and is also known as Euler's number.

a. Exponential function
b. Area hyperbolic functions
c. Integral part
d. ACTRAN

6. The terms 'dependent variable' and '_____' are used in similar but subtly different ways in mathematics and statistics as part of the standard terminology in those subjects. They are used to distinguish between two types of quantities being considered, separating them into those available at the start of a process and those being created by it, where the latter (dependent variables) are dependent on the former (independent variables.)

In traditional calculus, a function is defined as a relation between two terms called variables because their values vary.

a. Independent variable
b. ACTRAN
c. ALGOR
d. AUSM

7. In calculus, a branch of mathematics, the _____ is a measurement of how a function changes when its input changes. Loosely speaking, a _____ can be thought of as how much a quantity is changing at some given point. For example, the _____ of the position (or distance) of a vehicle with respect to time is the instantaneous velocity (respectively, instantaneous speed) at which the vehicle is traveling.

The process of finding a _____ is called differentiation. The fundamental theorem of calculus states that differentiation is the reverse process to integration.

    a. Derivative
    b. Semi-differentiability
    c. Bounded function
    d. Stationary phase approximation

8. In mathematics, the _____ is used to determine each point uniquely in a plane through two numbers, usually called the x-coordinate or abscissa and the y-coordinate or ordinate of the point. To define the coordinates, two perpendicular directed lines, are specified, as well as the unit length, which is marked off on the two axes Cartesian coordinate systems are also used in space and in higher dimensions.

    a. 15 theorem
    b. Cylindrical coordinate system
    c. Coordinate
    d. Cartesian coordinate system

9. In calculus, a method called _____ can be applied to implicitly defined functions. This method is an application of the chain rule allowing one to calculate the derivative of a function given implicitly.

As explained in the introduction, y can be given as a function of x implicitly rather than explicitly. When we have an equation R (x,y) = 0, we may be able to solve it for y and then differentiate. However, sometimes it is simpler to differentiate R(x,y) with respect to x and then solve for dy / dx.

    a. Implicit differentiation
    b. Implicit function
    c. Ordinary differential equation
    d. Automatic differentiation

10. In mathematics and its applications, a _____ system is a system for assigning an n-tuple of numbers or scalars to each point in an n-dimensional space. This concept is part of the theory of manifolds. 'Scalars' in many cases means real numbers, but, depending on context, can mean complex numbers or elements of some other commutative ring.

a. Coordinate
b. Cylindrical coordinate system
c. Spherical coordinate system
d. 15 theorem

11. In computer science and information science, _____ could also be a method or an algorithm. Again, an example will illustrate: There are systems of counting, as with Roman numerals, and various systems for filing papers, or catalogues, and various library systems, of which the Dewey Decimal _____ is an example. This still fits with the definition of components which are connected together (in this case in order to facilitate the flow of information.)
   a. BIBO stability
   b. BDDC
   c. 15 theorem
   d. System

12. When the number of variables is two, this is a _____, if it is three this is a level surface, and for higher values of n the level set is a level hypersurface.

More specifically, a _____ is the set of all real-valued roots of an equation in two variables x_1 and x_2. A level surface is the set of all real-valued roots of an equation in three variables x_1, x_2 and x_3.

   a. Partial derivative
   b. Scalar field
   c. Multipole moment
   d. Level curve

13. In mathematics, a (topological) _____ is defined as follows: let I be an interval of real numbers (i.e. a non-empty connected subset of $\mathbb{R}$); then a _____ γ is a continuous mapping $\gamma : I \to X$, where X is a topological space. The _____ γ is said to be simple if it is injective, i.e. if for all x, y in I, we have $\gamma(x) = \gamma(y) \implies x = y$. If I is a closed bounded interval $[a, b]$, we also allow the possibility $\gamma(a) = \gamma(b)$ (this convention makes it possible to talk about closed simple _____.)
   a. Prolate cycloid
   b. Tractrix
   c. Closed curve
   d. Curve

14. A _____ is a statement of the meaning of a word or phrase. The term to be defined is known as the definiendum. The words which define it are known as the definiens.

a. 15 theorem
b. BIBO stability
c. BDDC
d. Definition

15. In mathematics, a _____ of a function of several variables is its derivative with respect to one of those variables with the others held constant (as opposed to the total derivative, in which all variables are allowed to vary.) Partial derivatives are useful in vector calculus and differential geometry.

The _____ of a function f with respect to the variable x is written as f'_x, $\partial_x f$, or $\partial f/\partial x$.

a. Differentiation operator
b. Jacobian
c. Level curve
d. Partial Derivative

16. In economics, the _____ functional form of production functions is widely used to represent the relationship of an output to inputs. It was proposed by Knut Wicksell (1851-1926), and tested against statistical evidence by Charles Cobb and Paul Douglas in 1900-1928.

For production, the function is

$$Y = AL^\alpha K^\beta,$$

where:

- Y = total production (the monetary value of all goods produced in a year)
- L = labor input
- K = capital input
- A = total factor productivity
- α and β are the output elasticities of labor and capital, respectively. These values are constants determined by available technology.

Output elasticity measures the responsiveness of output to a change in levels of either labor or capital used in production, ceteris paribus. For example if α = 0.15, a 1% increase in labor would lead to approximately a 0.15% increase in output.

Chapter 8. Calculus of Several Variables

a. BIBO stability
b. BDDC
c. 15 theorem
d. Cobb-Douglas

17. The largest and the smallest element of a set are called extreme values, absolute extrema, or extreme records.

For a differentiable function f, if $f(x_0)$ is an _____ for the set of all values f(x), and if x_0 is in the interior of the domain of f, then x_0 is a critical point, by Fermat's theorem.

In the case of a general partial order one should not confuse a least element (smaller than all other) and a minimal element (nothing is smaller.)

a. Extreme value
b. Infinitesimal
c. Extreme Value Theorem
d. Integration by substitution

18. Integration is an important concept in mathematics, specifically in the field of calculus and, more broadly, mathematical analysis. Given a function f of a real variable x and an interval [a, b] of the real line, the _____

$$\int_a^b f(x)\, dx,$$

is defined informally to be the net signed area of the region in the xy-plane bounded by the graph of f, the x-axis, and the vertical lines x = a and x = b.

The term '_____' may also refer to the notion of antiderivative, a function F whose derivative is the given function f.

a. Indefinite integral
b. Integral
c. Integral test for convergence
d. Integrand

19. In mathematics, _____ and minima, known collectively as extrema, are the largest value (maximum) or smallest value (minimum), that a function takes in a point either within a given neighbourhood (local extremum) or on the function domain in its entirety (global extremum.)

Chapter 8. Calculus of Several Variables

Throughout, a point refers to an input (x), while a value refers to an output (y): one distinguishing between the maximum value and the point (or points) at which it occurs.

A real-valued function f defined on the real line is said to have a local maximum point at the point x^*, if there exists some $\varepsilon > 0$, such that $f(x^*) \geq f(x)$ when $|x - x^*| < \varepsilon$.

a. Maxima
b. Leibniz formula
c. Related rates
d. Racetrack principle

20. In a totally ordered set all elements are mutually comparable, so such a set can have at most one minimal element and at most one maximal element. Then, due to mutual comparability, the minimal element will also be the least element and the maximal element will also be the greatest element. Thus in a totally ordered set we can simply use the terms minimum and _____.

a. Nth term
b. Racetrack principle
c. Maximum
d. Leibniz rule

21. In a totally ordered set all elements are mutually comparable, so such a set can have at most one minimal element and at most one maximal element. Then, due to mutual comparability, the minimal element will also be the least element and the maximal element will also be the greatest element. Thus in a totally ordered set we can simply use the terms _____ and maximum.

a. Ghosts of departed quantities
b. Nth term
c. Maximum
d. Minimum

22. In mathematics, a _____ is a point in the domain of a function of two variables which is a stationary point but not a local extremum. At such a point, in general, the surface resembles a saddle that curves up in one direction, and curves down in a different direction (like a mountain pass.) In terms of contour lines, a _____ can be recognized, in general, by a contour that appears to intersect itself.

a. BIBO stability
b. BDDC
c. 15 theorem
d. Saddle point

23. In mathematics, a _____ (or critical number) is a point on the domain of a function where:

- one dimension: the derivative (or slope of the line when visualized) is equal to zero or a point where the function ceases to be differentiable.
- in general: there are two distinct concepts: either the derivative (Jacobian) vanishes, or it is not of full rank (or, in either case, the function is not differentiable); these agree in one dimension.

Note that in one dimension, a critical value or critical number x of function f is the domain element at which the derivative is zero or undefined, whereas the associated ordered pair (x, y) is the _____. In higher dimensions a critical value is in the range whereas a _____ is in the domain.

There are two situations in which a point becomes a _____ of a function of one variable. The first of which is that the value of the first derivative is equal to zero.

a. Differentiation operator
b. Multivariable calculus
c. Total derivative
d. Critical point

24. Let f be a differentiable function, and let f'(x) be its derivative. The derivative of f'(x) (if it has one) is written f''(x) and is called the _____ of f. Similarly, the derivative of a _____, if it exists, is written f'''(x) and is called the third derivative of f.

a. Stationary phase approximation
b. Vertical asymptote
c. Second Derivative
d. Slant asymptote

25. In calculus, a branch of mathematics, the _____ is a criterion often useful for determining whether a given stationary point of a function is a local maximum or a local minimum.

Chapter 8. Calculus of Several Variables

The test states: If the function f is twice differentiable at a stationary point x, meaning that $f'(x) = 0$, then:

- If $f''(x) < 0$ then f has a local maximum at x.
- If $f''(x) > 0$ then f has a local minimum at x.
- If $f''(x) = 0$, the _____ says nothing about the point x, has a possible inflection point.

In the last case, the function may have a local maximum or minimum there, but the function is sufficiently 'flat' that this is undetected by the second derivative. In this case one has to examine the third derivative. Such an example is f(x) = x⁴.

a. Symmetric derivative
b. Linearity of differentiation
c. Stationary point
d. Second Derivative Test

26. The function $\log_b(x)$ depends on both b and x, but the term _____ in standard usage refers to a function of the form $\log_b(x)$ in which the base b is fixed and so the only argument is x. Thus there is one _____ for each value of the base b (which must be positive and must differ from 1.) Viewed in this way, the base-b _____ is the inverse function of the exponential function b^x.

a. 15 theorem
b. Logarithm function
c. BIBO stability
d. BDDC

27. The method of _____ or ordinary _____ is used to solve overdetermined systems. _____ is often applied in statistical contexts, particularly regression analysis.

_____ can be interpreted as a method of fitting data. The best fit in the _____ sense is that instance of the model for which the sum of squared residuals has its least value, a residual being the difference between an observed value and the value given by the model.

a. Least squares
b. 15 theorem
c. BIBO stability
d. BDDC

Chapter 8. Calculus of Several Variables

28. A _____ is a 2D geometric symbolic representation of information according to some visualization technique. Sometimes, the technique uses a 3D visualization which is then projected onto the 2D surface.

_____ has two meanings in common sense.

a. BIBO stability
b. BDDC
c. 15 theorem
d. Diagram

29. A _____ is a type of display using Cartesian coordinates to display values for two variables for a set of data. The data is displayed as a collection of points, each having the value of one variable determining the position on the horizontal axis and the value of the other variable determining the position on the vertical axis.

a. Scatter plot
b. BDDC
c. 15 theorem
d. BIBO stability

30. In mathematics, a _____ (in one variable) is an infinite series of the form

$$f(x) = \sum_{n=0}^{\infty} a_n (x-c)^n = a_0 + a_1(x-c)^1 + a_2(x-c)^2 + a_3(x-c)^3 + \cdots$$

where a_n represents the coefficient of the nth term, c is a constant, and x varies around c (for this reason one sometimes speaks of the series as being centered at c

In many situations c is equal to zero, for instance when considering a Maclaurin series.

a. Stationary phase approximation
b. Differential calculus
c. Differential coefficient
d. Power series

31. In mathematics, the simplest case of _____ refers to the study of problems in which one seeks to minimize or maximize a real function by systematically choosing the values of real or integer variables from within an allowed set. This (a scalar real valued objective function) is actually a small subset of this field which comprises a large area of applied mathematics and generalizes to study of means to obtain 'best available' values of some objective function given a defined domain where the elaboration is on the types of functions and the conditions and nature of the objects in the problem domain.

The first _____ technique, which is known as steepest descent, goes back to Gauss.

   a. ACTRAN
   b. ALGOR
   c. AUSM
   d. Optimization

32. In infinitesimal calculus, a _____ is traditionally an infinitesimally small change in a variable. For example, if x is a variable, then a change in the value of x is often denoted Δx (or δx when this change is considered to be small.) The _____ dx represents such a change, but is infinitely small.
   a. The Method of Mechanical Theorems
   b. Local maximum
   c. Dirichlet integral
   d. Differential

33. Just as the definite integral of a positive function of one variable represents the area of the region between the graph of the function and the x-axis, the _____ of a positive function of two variables represents the volume of the region between the surface defined by the function (on the three dimensional Cartesian plane where z = f(x,y)) and the plane which contains its domain. (Note that the same volume can be obtained via the triple integral -- the integral of a function in three variables -- of the constant function f(x, y, z) = 1 over the above-mentioned region between the surface and the plane.) If there are more variables, a multiple integral will yield hypervolumes of multi-dimensional functions.
   a. Constant of integration
   b. Trigonometric substitution
   c. Risch algorithm
   d. Double integral

34. In mathematics, a _____ is a method for approximating the total area underneath a curve on a graph, otherwise known as an integral. It may also be used to define the integration operation.

Consider a function $f: D \rightarrow \mathbf{R}$, where D is a subset of the real numbers $\mathbf{R}$, and let $I = [a, b]$ be a closed interval contained in D. A finite set of points $\{x_0, x_1, x_2, ... x_n\}$ such that $a = x_0 < x_1 < x_2 ... < x_n = b$ creates a partition

$$P = \{[x_0, x_1), [x_1, x_2), ... [x_{n-1}, x_n]\}$$

of I.

a. Risch algorithm
b. Riemann sum
c. Solid of revolution
d. Signed measure

35. The _____ of any solid, liquid, plasma, vacuum or theoretical object is how much three-dimensional space it occupies, often quantified numerically. One-dimensional figures (such as lines) and two-dimensional shapes (such as squares) are assigned zero _____ in the three-dimensional space. _____ is commonly presented in units such as mL or cm^3 (milliliters or cubic centimeters.)
a. Dirac equation
b. Klein-Gordon equation
c. Volume
d. Vector potential

Chapter 9. Differential Equations

1. A _____ is a mathematical equation for an unknown function of one or several variables that relates the values of the function itself and of its derivatives of various orders. they play a prominent role in engineering, physics, economics and other disciplines.

A simplified real world example of a _____ is modeling the acceleration of a ball falling through the air (considering only gravity and air resistance.)

   a. Structural stability
   b. Caloric polynomial
   c. Phase line
   d. Differential equation

2. In calculus, a branch of mathematics, the _____ is a measurement of how a function changes when its input changes. Loosely speaking, a _____ can be thought of as how much a quantity is changing at some given point. For example, the _____ of the position (or distance) of a vehicle with respect to time is the instantaneous velocity (respectively, instantaneous speed) at which the vehicle is traveling.

The process of finding a _____ is called differentiation. The fundamental theorem of calculus states that differentiation is the reverse process to integration.

   a. Semi-differentiability
   b. Bounded function
   c. Derivative
   d. Stationary phase approximation

3. In mathematics, a (topological) _____ is defined as follows: let I be an interval of real numbers (i.e. a non-empty connected subset of $\mathbb{R}$); then a _____ γ is a continuous mapping $\gamma : I \to X$, where X is a topological space. The _____ γ is said to be simple if it is injective, i.e. if for all x, y in I, we have $\gamma(x) = \gamma(y) \implies x = y$. If I is a closed bounded interval $[a, b]$, we also allow the possibility $\gamma(a) = \gamma(b)$ (this convention makes it possible to talk about closed simple _____.)
   a. Closed curve
   b. Prolate cycloid
   c. Tractrix
   d. Curve

4. A _____ in biology generally concerns a measured property such as population size, body height or biomass. Values for the measured property can be plotted on a graph as a function of time.

a. Cauchy-Euler equation
b. Spectral theory of ordinary differential equations
c. Variation of parameters
d. Growth curve

5. The _____ of a quantity whose value decreases with time is the interval required for the quantity to decay to half of its initial value. The concept originated in describing how long it takes atoms to undergo radioactive decay but also applies in a wide variety of other situations.

The term '_____' dates to 1907.

a. BDDC
b. 15 theorem
c. BIBO stability
d. Half-life

6. In acoustics and telecommunication, a _____ of a wave is a component frequency of the signal that is an integer multiple of the fundamental frequency. For example, if the fundamental frequency is f, the harmonics have frequencies f, 2f, 3f, 4f, etc. The harmonics have the property that they are all periodic at the fundamental frequency, therefore the sum of harmonics is also periodic at that frequency.
a. BIBO stability
b. 15 theorem
c. BDDC
d. Harmonic

7. In mathematics, the _____ is the infinite series

$$\sum_{k=1}^{\infty} \frac{1}{k} = 1 + \frac{1}{2} + \frac{1}{3} + \frac{1}{4} + \cdots.$$

Its name derives from the concept of overtones, or harmonics, in music: the wavelengths of the overtones of a vibrating string are 1/2, 1/3, 1/4, etc., of the string's fundamental wavelength. Every term of the series after the first is the harmonic mean of the neighboring terms; the term harmonic mean likewise derives from music.

The _____ diverges to infinity, albeit rather slowly (the first 10^{43} terms sum to less than 100 .)

a. Harmonic series
b. BDDC
c. 15 theorem
d. BIBO stability

8. In mathematics, _____ is any of several methods for solving ordinary and partial differential equations, in which algebra allows one to rewrite an equation so that each of two variables occurs on a different side of the equation.

Suppose a differential equation can be written in the form

$$\frac{d}{dx}f(x) = g(x)h(f(x)), \qquad (1)$$

which we can write more simply by letting y = f(x):

$$\frac{dy}{dx} = g(x)h(y).$$

As long as h(y) ≠ 0, we can rearrange terms to obtain:

$$\frac{dy}{h(y)} = g(x)dx,$$

so that the two variables x and y have been separated.

Some who dislike Leibniz's notation may prefer to write this as

$$\frac{1}{h(y)}\frac{dy}{dx} = g(x),$$

but that fails to make it quite as obvious why this is called '_____'.

a. Power series method
b. Damping ratio
c. Sturm separation theorem
d. Separation of variables

Chapter 9. Differential Equations

9. In mathematics, a _____ differential equation may refer to one of two related things, both of which are differential equations that can be attacked by a method of separation of variables.

- For ordinary differential equations, it describes a class of equations that can be separated into a pair of integrals. See: Examples of differential equations

- For partial differential equations, it describes a class of equations that can be broken down into differential equations in fewer independent variables. See _____ partial differential equation.

   a. Differential equation
   b. Method of undetermined coefficients
   c. Lax pair
   d. Separable

10. In mathematics, in the field of differential equations, an _____ is an ordinary differential equation together with specified value, called the initial condition, of the unknown function at a given point in the domain of the solution. In physics or other sciences, modeling a system frequently amounts to solving an _____; in this context, the differential equation is an evolution equation specifying how, given initial conditions, the system will evolve with time.

An _____ is a differential equation

$$y'(t) = f(t, y(t)) \quad \text{with} \quad f : \mathbb{R} \times \mathbb{R} \to \mathbb{R}$$

together with a point in the domain of f

$$(t_0, y_0) \in \mathbb{R} \times \mathbb{R},$$

called the initial condition.

   a. ACTRAN
   b. ALGOR
   c. AUSM
   d. Initial value problem

11. _____ is a type of motion in which the velocity of an object changes equal amounts in equal time periods. An example of an object having _____ would be a ball rolling down a ramp. The object picks up velocity as it goes down the ramp with equal changes in time.

a. Uniform Acceleration
b. AUSM
c. ACTRAN
d. ALGOR

12. A _____ officer is an officer of high military rank. The term or equivalent is used by nearly every country in the world. _____ can be used as a generic term for all grades of _____ officer, or it can specifically refer to a single rank that is just called _____.
    a. 15 theorem
    b. BIBO stability
    c. BDDC
    d. General

13. In mathematics, a _____ to an ordinary or partial differential equation is a function for which the derivatives appearing in the equation may not all exist but which is nonetheless deemed to satisfy the equation in some precisely defined sense. There are many different definitions of _____, appropriate for different classes of equations. One of the most important is based on the notion of distributions.
    a. Conserved quantity
    b. Weak solution
    c. Structural stability
    d. Singular perturbation

Chapter 10. Probability and Calculus

1. _____ is a way of expressing knowledge or belief that an event will occur or has occurred. In mathematics the concept has been given an exact meaning in _____ theory, that is used extensively in such areas of study as mathematics, statistics, finance, gambling, science, and philosophy to draw conclusions about the likelihood of potential events and the underlying mechanics of complex systems.

The word _____ does not have a consistent direct definition.

   a. Probability
   b. Discrete probability distributions
   c. Linear regression
   d. Normal distribution

2. In calculus, _____ is a tool for finding antiderivatives and integrals. Using the fundamental theorem of calculus often requires finding an antiderivative. For this and other reasons, _____ is a relatively important tool for mathematicians.
   a. Integration by substitution
   b. Extreme value
   c. Odd function
   d. Integral of secant cubed

3. The method of _____ or ordinary _____ is used to solve overdetermined systems. _____ is often applied in statistical contexts, particularly regression analysis.

_____ can be interpreted as a method of fitting data. The best fit in the _____ sense is that instance of the model for which the sum of squared residuals has its least value, a residual being the difference between an observed value and the value given by the model.

   a. Least squares
   b. 15 theorem
   c. BIBO stability
   d. BDDC

4. In mathematics, a _____ is a function for which, intuitively, small changes in the input result in small changes in the output. Otherwise, a function is said to be discontinuous. A _____ with a continuous inverse function is called bicontinuous. An intuitive though imprecise (and inexact) idea of continuity is given by the common statement that a _____ is a function whose graph can be drawn without lifting the chalk from the blackboard.

a. Binomial series
b. Continuous function
c. Hyperbolic angle
d. Visual Calculus

5. In vector calculus, the _____ is an operator that measures the magnitude of a vector field's source or sink at a given point; the _____ of a vector field is a (signed) scalar. For example, consider air as it is heated or cooled. The relevant vector field for this example is the velocity of the moving air at a point.
   a. Triple product
   b. Green's theorem
   c. Gradient theorem
   d. Divergence

6. In probability theory, a probability distribution is called continuous if its cumulative distribution function is continuous. This is equivalent to saying that for random variables X with the distribution in question, Pr[X = a] = 0 for all real numbers a, i.e.: the probability that X attains the value a is zero, for any number a. If the distribution of X is continuous then X is called a _____.
   a. Probability
   b. Standard deviation
   c. Poisson distribution
   d. Continuous random variable

7. The _____ of a material is defined as its mass per unit volume. The symbol of _____ is ρ '>rho.)

Mathematically:

$$d = \frac{m}{V}$$

where:

d is the _____,
m is the mass,
V is the volume.

Chapter 10. Probability and Calculus

a. BIBO stability
b. Density
c. 15 theorem
d. BDDC

8. In mathematics, a probability _____ is a function that represents a probability distribution in terms of integrals.

Formally, a probability distribution has density f, if f is a non-negative Lebesgue-integrable function $\mathbb{R} \to \mathbb{R}$ such that the probability of the interval [a, b] is given by

$$\int_a^b f(x)\,dx$$

for any two numbers a and b. This implies that the total integral of f must be 1.

a. 15 theorem
b. Factorial moment generating function
c. BDDC
d. Density function

9. The _____ are a pair of first order, non-linear, differential equations frequently used to describe the dynamics of biological systems in which two species interact, one a predator and one its prey. They were proposed independently by Alfred J. Lotka in 1925 and Vito Volterra in 1926.

where

- y is the number of some predator;
- x is the number of its prey;
- dy/dt and dx/dt represents the growth of the two populations against time;
- t represents the time; and
- >α, >β, >γ and >δ are parameters representing the interaction of the two species.

When multiplied out, the equations take a form useful for physical interpretation. Their origin should be considered from a more general framework,

where both functions represent per capita growth rates of the prey and predator, respectively.

   a. BIBO stability
   b. BDDC
   c. 15 theorem
   d. Lotka-Volterra equations

10. _____ is a type of motion in which the velocity of an object changes equal amounts in equal time periods. An example of an object having _____ would be a ball rolling down a ramp. The object picks up velocity as it goes down the ramp with equal changes in time.
   a. ACTRAN
   b. AUSM
   c. Uniform Acceleration
   d. ALGOR

11. In mathematics, a _____ (pdf) is a function that represents a probability distribution in terms of integrals.

Formally, a probability distribution has density f, if f is a non-negative Lebesgue-integrable function $\mathbb{R} \to \mathbb{R}$ such that the probability of the interval [a, b] is given by

$$\int_a^b f(x)\,dx$$

for any two numbers a and b. This implies that the total integral of f must be 1.

   a. BDDC
   b. 15 theorem
   c. Probability density function
   d. Factorial moment generating function

Chapter 10. Probability and Calculus

12. In probability theory and statistics, the _____ (or expectation value or mean and for continuous random variables with a density function it is the probability density -weighted integral of the possible values.

The term '_____' can be misleading.

   a. ACTRAN
   b. ALGOR
   c. AUSM
   d. Expected value

13. In statistics, _____ is a simple measure of the variability or dispersion of a data set. A low _____ indicates that all of the data points are very close to the same value (the mean), while high _____ indicates that the data is 'spread out' over a large range of values.

For example, the average height for adult men in the United States is about 70 inches, with a _____ of around 3 inches.

   a. Continuous random variable
   b. Standard deviation
   c. Correlation
   d. Poisson distribution

14. The _____ is an important family of continuous probability distributions, applicable in many fields. Each member of the family may be defined by two parameters, location and scale: the mean and variance respectively. The standard _____ is the _____ with a mean of zero and a variance of one.

   a. Normal distribution
   b. Moment
   c. Correlation
   d. Continuous random variable

15. In mathematics, a (topological) _____ is defined as follows: let I be an interval of real numbers (i.e. a non-empty connected subset of $\mathbb{R}$); then a _____ γ is a continuous mapping $\gamma : I \to X$, where X is a topological space. The _____ γ is said to be simple if it is injective, i.e. if for all x, y in I, we have $\gamma(x) = \gamma(y) \implies x = y$. If I is a closed bounded interval $[a, b]$, we also allow the possibility $\gamma(a) = \gamma(b)$ (this convention makes it possible to talk about closed simple _____.)

a. Tractrix
b. Closed curve
c. Curve
d. Prolate cycloid

Chapter 11. Taylor Polynomials and Infinite Series

1. In calculus, _____ gives a sequence of approximations of a differentiable function around a given point by polynomials (the Taylor polynomials of that function) whose coefficients depend only on the derivatives of the function at that point. The theorem also gives precise estimates on the size of the error in the approximation. The theorem is named after the mathematician Brook Taylor, who stated it in 1712, though the result was first discovered 41 years earlier in 1671 by James Gregory.
   a. Related rates
   b. Fresnel integrals
   c. Local minimum
   d. Taylor's theorem

2. Cantor defined two kinds of _____ numbers, the ordinal numbers and the cardinal numbers. Ordinal numbers may be identified with well-ordered sets, or counting carried on to any stopping point, including points after an _____ number have already been counted. Generalizing finite and the ordinary _____ sequences which are maps from the positive integers leads to mappings from ordinal numbers, and transfinite sequences.
   a. ALGOR
   b. ACTRAN
   c. AUSM
   d. Infinite

3. The terms of the series are often produced according to a certain rule, such as by a formula, by an algorithm, by a sequence of measurements, or even by a random number generator. As there are an infinite number of terms, this notion is often called an _____. Unlike finite summations, series need tools from mathematical analysis to be fully understood and manipulated.
   a. Integration by substitution
   b. Extreme Value Theorem
   c. Extreme value
   d. Infinite series

4. In mathematics, a _____ is an ordered list of objects (or events). Like a set, it contains members (also called elements or terms), and the number of terms (possibly infinite) is called the length of the _____. Unlike a set, order matters, and the exact same elements can appear multiple times at different positions in the _____.
   a. Y-intercept
   b. Sequence
   c. Slope
   d. 15 theorem

5. A _____ officer is an officer of high military rank. The term or equivalent is used by nearly every country in the world. _____ can be used as a generic term for all grades of _____ officer, or it can specifically refer to a single rank that is just called _____.

a. 15 theorem
b. BDDC
c. BIBO stability
d. General

6. In calculus, an _____ is the limit of a definite integral as an endpoint of the interval of integration approaches either a specified real number or ∞ or −∞ or, in some cases, as both endpoints approach limits.

Specifically, an _____ is a limit of the form

$$\lim_{b\to\infty} \int_a^b f(x)\,dx, \qquad \lim_{a\to-\infty} \int_a^b f(x)\,dx,$$

or of the form

$$\lim_{c\to b^-} \int_a^c f(x)\,dx, \qquad \lim_{c\to a^+} \int_c^b f(x)\,dx,$$

in which one takes a limit in one or the other (or sometimes both) endpoints. Improper integrals may also occur at an interior point of the domain of integration, or at multiple such points.

a. AUSM
b. ACTRAN
c. ALGOR
d. Improper integral

7. A _____, in mathematics, is a polynomial function of the form $f(x) = ax^2 + bx + c$, where $a \neq 0$. The graph of a _____ is a parabola whose major axis is parallel to the y-axis.

The expression ax² + bx + c in the definition of a _____ is a polynomial of degree 2 or a 2nd degree polynomial, because the highest exponent of x is 2.

a. Leading coefficient
b. Resultant
c. Discriminant
d. Quadratic function

8. Integration is an important concept in mathematics, specifically in the field of calculus and, more broadly, mathematical analysis. Given a function f of a real variable x and an interval [a, b] of the real line, the _____

$$\int_a^b f(x)\, dx,$$

is defined informally to be the net signed area of the region in the xy-plane bounded by the graph of f, the x-axis, and the vertical lines x = a and x = b.

The term '_____' may also refer to the notion of antiderivative, a function F whose derivative is the given function f.

a. Integrand
b. Integral
c. Integral test for convergence
d. Indefinite integral

9. In mathematics, the concept of a '_____' is used to describe the behavior of a function as its argument or input either 'gets close' to some point, or as the argument becomes arbitrarily large; or the behavior of a sequence's elements as their index increases indefinitely. Limits are used in calculus and other branches of mathematical analysis to define derivatives and continuity.

In formulas, _____ is usually abbreviated as lim

a. Limit
b. BDDC
c. 15 theorem
d. BIBO stability

10. Call S_N the _____ to N of the sequence $\{a_n\}$, or _____ of the series. A series is the sequence of partial sums, $\{S_N\}$.

When talking about series, one can refer either to the sequence $\{S_N\}$ of the partial sums, or to the sum of the series,

$$\sum_{n=0}^{\infty} a_n$$

i.e., the limit of the sequence of partial sums - it is clear which one is meant from context.

a. The Method of Mechanical Theorems
b. Maxima
c. Dirichlet integral
d. Partial sum

11. In mathematics, a _____ is an infinite series that is not convergent, meaning that the infinite sequence of the partial sums of the series does not have a limit.

If a series converges, the individual terms of the series must approach zero. Thus any series in which the individual terms do not approach zero diverges.

a. BIBO stability
b. BDDC
c. 15 theorem
d. Divergent Series

12. In mathematics, a _____ is a series with a constant ratio between successive terms. For example, the series

$$\frac{1}{2} + \frac{1}{4} + \frac{1}{8} + \frac{1}{16} + \cdots$$

is geometric, because each term is equal to half of the previous term. The sum of this series is 1, as illustrated in the following picture:

_____ are one of the simplest examples of infinite series with finite sums.

a. Sequence transformation
b. Conditionally convergent
c. Geometric series
d. Converge absolutely

13. In calculus, a method called _____ can be applied to implicitly defined functions. This method is an application of the chain rule allowing one to calculate the derivative of a function given implicitly.

As explained in the introduction, y can be given as a function of x implicitly rather than explicitly. When we have an equation R(x,y) = 0, we may be able to solve it for y and then differentiate. However, sometimes it is simpler to differentiate R(x,y) with respect to x and then solve for dy / dx.

a. Implicit function
b. Implicit differentiation
c. Ordinary differential equation
d. Automatic differentiation

14. In calculus, a branch of mathematics, the _____ is a measurement of how a function changes when its input changes. Loosely speaking, a _____ can be thought of as how much a quantity is changing at some given point. For example, the _____ of the position (or distance) of a vehicle with respect to time is the instantaneous velocity (respectively, instantaneous speed) at which the vehicle is traveling.

The process of finding a _____ is called differentiation. The fundamental theorem of calculus states that differentiation is the reverse process to integration.

a. Bounded function
b. Semi-differentiability
c. Derivative
d. Stationary phase approximation

15. In acoustics and telecommunication, a _____ of a wave is a component frequency of the signal that is an integer multiple of the fundamental frequency. For example, if the fundamental frequency is f, the harmonics have frequencies f, 2f, 3f, 4f, etc. The harmonics have the property that they are all periodic at the fundamental frequency, therefore the sum of harmonics is also periodic at that frequency.
a. BDDC
b. 15 theorem
c. BIBO stability
d. Harmonic

16. In mathematics, the _____ is the infinite series

$$\sum_{k=1}^{\infty} \frac{1}{k} = 1 + \frac{1}{2} + \frac{1}{3} + \frac{1}{4} + \cdots.$$

Its name derives from the concept of overtones, or harmonics, in music: the wavelengths of the overtones of a vibrating string are 1/2, 1/3, 1/4, etc., of the string's fundamental wavelength. Every term of the series after the first is the harmonic mean of the neighboring terms; the term harmonic mean likewise derives from music.

The _____ diverges to infinity, albeit rather slowly (the first 10^{43} terms sum to less than 100 .)

a. 15 theorem
b. BDDC
c. BIBO stability
d. Harmonic series

17. In vector calculus, the _____ is an operator that measures the magnitude of a vector field's source or sink at a given point; the _____ of a vector field is a (signed) scalar. For example, consider air as it is heated or cooled. The relevant vector field for this example is the velocity of the moving air at a point.
    a. Divergence
    b. Green's theorem
    c. Gradient theorem
    d. Triple product

18. In mathematics, the nth term _____ is a simple test for the divergence of an infinite series:

- If $\lim_{n \to \infty} a_n \neq 0$ or if the limit does not exist, then $\sum_{n=1}^{\infty} a_n$ diverges.

Many authors do not name this test or give it a shorter name.

Unlike stronger convergence tests, the term test cannot prove by itself that a series converges. In particular, the converse to the test is not true; instead all one can say is:

- If $\lim_{n \to \infty} a_n = 0$, then $\sum_{n=1}^{\infty} a_n$ may or may not converge. In other words, if $\lim_{n \to \infty} a_n = 0$, the test is inconclusive.

The harmonic series is a classic example of a divergent series whose terms limit to zero. The more general class of p-series,

$$\sum_{n=1}^{\infty} \frac{1}{n^p},$$

Chapter 11. Taylor Polynomials and Infinite Series

exemplifies the possible results of the test:

- If p ≤ 0, then the term test identifies the series as divergent.
- If 0 < p ≤ 1, then the term test is inconclusive, but the series is divergent by the integral test for convergence.
- If 1 < p, then the term test is inconclusive, but the series is convergent, again by the integral test for convergence.

The test is typically proved in contrapositive form:

- If $\sum_{n=1}^{\infty} a_n$ converges, then $\lim_{n \to \infty} a_n = 0.$

If s_n are the partial sums of the series, then the assumption that the series converges means that

$$\lim_{n \to \infty} s_n = s$$

for some number s. Then

$$\lim_{n \to \infty} a_n = \lim_{n \to \infty} (s_n - s_{n-1}) = s - s = 0.$$

The assumption that the series converges means that it passes Cauchy's convergence test: for every $\varepsilon > 0$ there is a number N such that

$$|a_{n+1} + a_{n+2} + \ldots + a_{n+p}| < \varepsilon$$

holds for all n > N and p ≥ 1. Setting p = 1 recovers the definition of the statement

$$\lim_{n \to \infty} a_n = 0.$$

The simplest version of the term test applies to infinite series of real numbers.

a. Leibniz differential
b. Fundamental Theorem of Calculus
c. Test for divergence
d. Calculus controversy

19. In mathematics, the _____ for convergence is a method used to test infinite series of non-negative terms for convergence. An early form of the test of convergence was developed in India by Madhava in the 14th century, and by his followers at the Kerala School. In Europe, it was later developed by Maclaurin and Cauchy and is sometimes known as the Maclaurin-Cauchy test.

   a. Integral test
   b. AUSM
   c. ALGOR
   d. ACTRAN

20. In mathematics, the _____, sometimes called the direct _____ is a criterion for convergence or divergence of a series whose terms are real or complex numbers. The test determines convergence by comparing the terms of the series in question with those of a series whose convergence properties are known.

The _____ states that if the series

$$\sum_{n=1}^{\infty} b_n$$

is an absolutely convergent series and

$$|a_n| \leq |b_n|$$

for sufficiently large n , then the series

$$\sum_{n=1}^{\infty} a_n$$

converges absolutely.

   a. Comparison test
   b. Telescoping series
   c. Ratio test
   d. Conditionally convergent

21. In mathematics, the _____ of a power series is a non-negative quantity, either a real number or ∞, that represents a domain (within the radius) in which the series will converge. Within the _____, a power series converges absolutely and uniformly on compacta as well. If the series converges, it is the Taylor series of the analytic function to which it converges inside its _____.

Chapter 11. Taylor Polynomials and Infinite Series

a. Radius of convergence
b. Branch point
c. Holomorphically separable
d. Blaschke product

22. In mathematics, the _____ is a representation of a function as an infinite sum of terms calculated from the values of its derivatives at a single point. It may be regarded as the limit of the Taylor polynomials. If the series is centered at zero, the series is also called a Maclaurin series.
   a. BIBO stability
   b. Taylor series
   c. 15 theorem
   d. BDDC

23. In mathematics, a _____ (in one variable) is an infinite series of the form

$$f(x) = \sum_{n=0}^{\infty} a_n (x-c)^n = a_0 + a_1(x-c)^1 + a_2(x-c)^2 + a_3(x-c)^3 + \cdots$$

where a_n represents the coefficient of the nth term, c is a constant, and x varies around c (for this reason one sometimes speaks of the series as being centered at c

In many situations c is equal to zero, for instance when considering a Maclaurin series.

   a. Stationary phase approximation
   b. Differential calculus
   c. Differential coefficient
   d. Power series

Chapter 12. Trigonometric Functions

1. In mathematics, a _____ is a circle with a unit radius, i.e., a circle whose radius is 1. Frequently, especially in trigonometry, 'the' _____ is the circle of radius 1 centered at the origin (0, 0) in the Cartesian coordinate system in the Euclidean plane. The _____ is often denoted S^1; the generalization to higher dimensions is the unit sphere.
   a. Unit circle
   b. ACTRAN
   c. AUSM
   d. ALGOR

2. The _____ of an angle is the ratio of the length of the adjacent side to the length of the hypotenuse. In our case

$$\cos A = \frac{\text{adjacent}}{\text{hypotenuse}} = \frac{b}{h}.$$

The tangent of an angle is the ratio of the length of the opposite side to the length of the adjacent side. In our case

$$\tan A = \frac{\text{opposite}}{\text{adjacent}} = \frac{a}{b}.$$

The remaining three functions are best defined using the above three functions.

   a. Trigonometric
   b. Cosine
   c. Sine integral
   d. Trigonometric functions

3. The _____ of an angle is the ratio of the length of the opposite side to the length of the hypotenuse. In our case

$$\sin A = \frac{\text{opposite}}{\text{hypotenuse}} = \frac{a}{h}.$$

Note that this ratio does not depend on size of the particular right triangle chosen, as long as it contains the angle A, since all such triangles are similar.

The cosine of an angle is the ratio of the length of the adjacent side to the length of the hypotenuse.

a. Sine integral
b. Trigonometric
c. Trigonometric functions
d. Sine

4. In geometry, the _____ (or simply the tangent) to a curve at a given point is the straight line that 'just touches' the curve at that point (in the sense explained more precisely below.) As it passes through the point of tangency, the _____ is 'going in the same direction' as the curve, and in this sense it is the best straight-line approximation to the curve at that point. The same definition applies to space curves and curves in n-dimensional Euclidean space.
   a. North pole
   b. Tangent line
   c. Lie derivative
   d. Minimal surface

5. Trigonometry is a branch of mathematics that deals with triangles, particularly those plane triangles in which one angle has 90 degrees (right triangles.) Trigonometry deals with relationships between the sides and the angles of triangles and with the _____ functions, which describe those relationships.

Trigonometry has applications in both pure mathematics and in applied mathematics, where it is essential in many branches of science and technology.

   a. Sine
   b. Trigonometric integrals
   c. Trigonometric functions
   d. Trigonometric

6. In mathematics, the _____ are functions of an angle. They are important in the study of triangles and modeling periodic phenomena, among many other applications. _____ are commonly defined as ratios of two sides of a right triangle containing the angle, and can equivalently be defined as the lengths of various line segments from a unit circle.
   a. Trigonometric integrals
   b. Trigonometric functions
   c. Sine integral
   d. Trigonometric

7. The _____ are a pair of first order, non-linear, differential equations frequently used to describe the dynamics of biological systems in which two species interact, one a predator and one its prey. They were proposed independently by Alfred J. Lotka in 1925 and Vito Volterra in 1926.

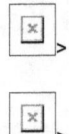

where

- y is the number of some predator;
- x is the number of its prey;
- dy/dt and dx/dt represents the growth of the two populations against time;
- t represents the time; and
- >α, >β, >γ and >δ are parameters representing the interaction of the two species.

When multiplied out, the equations take a form useful for physical interpretation. Their origin should be considered from a more general framework,

where both functions represent per capita growth rates of the prey and predator, respectively.

a. BIBO stability
b. BDDC
c. 15 theorem
d. Lotka-Volterra equations

8. The _____ of a material is defined as its mass per unit volume. The symbol of _____ is ρ '>rho.)

Mathematically:

$$d = \frac{m}{V}$$

where:

    d is the _____,
    m is the mass,
    V is the volume.

a. BDDC
b. 15 theorem
c. BIBO stability
d. Density

9. In mathematics, a probability _____ is a function that represents a probability distribution in terms of integrals.

Formally, a probability distribution has density f, if f is a non-negative Lebesgue-integrable function $\mathbb{R} \to \mathbb{R}$ such that the probability of the interval [a, b] is given by

$$\int_a^b f(x)\, dx$$

for any two numbers a and b. This implies that the total integral of f must be 1.

a. 15 theorem
b. Factorial moment generating function
c. BDDC
d. Density function

10. _____ is a way of expressing knowledge or belief that an event will occur or has occurred. In mathematics the concept has been given an exact meaning in _____ theory, that is used extensively in such areas of study as mathematics, statistics, finance, gambling, science, and philosophy to draw conclusions about the likelihood of potential events and the underlying mechanics of complex systems.

The word _____ does not have a consistent direct definition.

a. Probability
b. Normal distribution
c. Linear regression
d. Discrete probability distributions

11. In mathematics, a _____ (pdf) is a function that represents a probability distribution in terms of integrals.

Formally, a probability distribution has density f, if f is a non-negative Lebesgue-integrable function $\mathbb{R} \to \mathbb{R}$ such that the probability of the interval [a, b] is given by

$$\int_a^b f(x)\,dx$$

for any two numbers a and b. This implies that the total integral of f must be 1.

    a. Factorial moment generating function
    b. 15 theorem
    c. Probability density function
    d. BDDC

12. In mathematics, _____ are equalities that involve trigonometric functions that are true for every single value of the occurring variables. These identities are useful whenever expressions involving trigonometric functions need to be simplified. An important application is the integration of non-trigonometric functions: a common technique involves first using the substitution rule with a trigonometric function, and then simplifying the resulting integral with a trigonometric identity.

    a. 15 theorem
    b. BIBO stability
    c. Trigonometric identities
    d. BDDC

13. In calculus, a branch of mathematics, the _____ is a measurement of how a function changes when its input changes. Loosely speaking, a _____ can be thought of as how much a quantity is changing at some given point. For example, the _____ of the position (or distance) of a vehicle with respect to time is the instantaneous velocity (respectively, instantaneous speed) at which the vehicle is traveling.

The process of finding a _____ is called differentiation. The fundamental theorem of calculus states that differentiation is the reverse process to integration.

    a. Stationary phase approximation
    b. Derivative
    c. Bounded function
    d. Semi-differentiability

14. In mathematics, the trigonometric integrals are a family of integrals which involve trigonometric functions. A number of the basic trigonometric integrals are discussed at the list of integrals of trigonometric functions. Plot of Si(x) for $0 \leq x \leq 8\pi$.

The different _____ definitions are:

$$\text{Si}(x) = \int_0^x \frac{\sin t}{t}\, dt$$

$$\text{si}(x) = -\int_x^\infty \frac{\sin t}{t}\, dt$$

Si(x) is the primitive of sinx / x which is zero for x = 0; si(x) is the primitive of sinx / x which is zero for $x = \infty$.

a. Sine integral
b. Trigonometric functions
c. Trigonometric integrals
d. Sine

15. Integration is an important concept in mathematics, specifically in the field of calculus and, more broadly, mathematical analysis. Given a function f of a real variable x and an interval [a, b] of the real line, the _____

$$\int_a^b f(x)\, dx,$$

is defined informally to be the net signed area of the region in the xy-plane bounded by the graph of f, the x-axis, and the vertical lines x = a and x = b.

The term '_____' may also refer to the notion of antiderivative, a function F whose derivative is the given function f.

a. Integral test for convergence
b. Integrand
c. Indefinite integral
d. Integral

16. In mathematics, the _____ of a function y = f(x) is a function that, in some fashion, 'undoes' the effect of f The _____ of f is denoted f⁻¹. The statements y=f(x) and x=f⁻¹(y) are equivalent.

a. ACTRAN
b. AUSM
c. ALGOR
d. Inverse

17. In mathematics, if f is a function from A to B then an _____ for f is a function in the opposite direction, from B to A, with the property that a round trip (a composition) from A to B to A (or from B to A to B) returns each element of the initial set to itself. Thus, if an input x into the function f produces an output y, then inputting y into the _____ f^{-1} (read f inverse, not to be confused with exponentiation) produces the output x. Not every function has an inverse; those that do are called invertible.

a. Augustin-Jean Fresnel
b. Inverse function
c. Aristotle
d. Augustin Louis Cauchy

18. This article will state and prove the _____ for differentiation, and then use it to prove these two formulas.

The _____ for differentiation states that for every natural number n, the derivative of $f(x) = x^n$ is $f'(x) = nx^{n-1}$, that is,

$$(x^n)' = nx^{n-1}.$$

The _____ for integration

$$\int x^n \, dx = \frac{x^{n+1}}{n+1} + C$$

for natural n is then an easy consequence. One just needs to take the derivative of this equality and use the _____ and linearity of differentiation on the right-hand side.

a. Test for Divergence
b. Leibniz rule
c. Power Rule
d. Functional integration

19. In mathematics, the _____ is a test used to determine if a function is injective, surjective or bijective.

Chapter 12. Trigonometric Functions

Suppose there is a function f : X → Y with a graph., and you have a horizontal line of X x Y :
$y_0 \in Y, \{(x, y_0) : x \in X\} = (X \times y_0)$.

- If the function is injective, then it can be visualized as one whose graph is never intersected by any horizontal line more than once.
- If and only if f is surjective, any horizontal line will intersect the graph at least at one point (when the horizontal line is in the codomain.)
- If f is bijective, any horizontal line will intersect the graph at exactly one point.

This test is also used to find whether or not the inverse of the function is indeed a function as well. This is due to the reflective properties of the function over y=x.

a. 15 theorem
b. BDDC
c. BIBO stability
d. Horizontal line test

20. A _____ officer is an officer of high military rank. The term or equivalent is used by nearly every country in the world. _____ can be used as a generic term for all grades of _____ officer, or it can specifically refer to a single rank that is just called _____.
   a. BIBO stability
   b. 15 theorem
   c. BDDC
   d. General

ANSWER KEY

Chapter 1
1. d 2. d 3. a 4. a 5. b 6. d 7. d 8. d 9. a 10. d
11. d 12. d 13. c 14. c 15. a 16. d

Chapter 2
1. d 2. d 3. a 4. c 5. d 6. d 7. d 8. b 9. d 10. b
11. d 12. d 13. b 14. b 15. d 16. b 17. d 18. c 19. c 20. d
21. a 22. d 23. a 24. d 25. a 26. a 27. d 28. b 29. d 30. b
31. d 32. d 33. b 34. b 35. c 36. d 37. d 38. b 39. d 40. d

Chapter 3
1. d 2. d 3. d 4. a 5. d 6. d 7. d 8. a 9. c 10. a
11. d 12. c 13. d 14. d 15. a 16. d 17. b 18. a 19. a 20. b
21. d 22. d 23. d

Chapter 4
1. d 2. a 3. d 4. d 5. b 6. b 7. d 8. a 9. c 10. a
11. c 12. d 13. a 14. b 15. d 16. d 17. b 18. d 19. c 20. d
21. d

Chapter 5
1. a 2. b 3. c 4. b 5. d 6. b 7. d 8. d 9. d 10. d
11. d 12. b 13. b 14. d 15. d 16. a 17. d 18. d 19. d 20. a
21. b 22. d 23. d

Chapter 6
1. d 2. a 3. b 4. a 5. d 6. a 7. a 8. d 9. d 10. a
11. d 12. d 13. b 14. b 15. c 16. d 17. b 18. c 19. a 20. a
21. d 22. d 23. d 24. d 25. d

Chapter 7
1. d 2. b 3. d 4. d 5. c

Chapter 8
1. d 2. d 3. d 4. b 5. a 6. a 7. a 8. d 9. a 10. a
11. d 12. d 13. d 14. d 15. d 16. d 17. a 18. b 19. a 20. c
21. d 22. d 23. d 24. c 25. d 26. b 27. a 28. d 29. a 30. d
31. d 32. d 33. d 34. b 35. c

Chapter 9
1. d 2. c 3. d 4. d 5. d 6. d 7. a 8. d 9. d 10. d
11. a 12. d 13. b

Chapter 10
1. a 2. a 3. a 4. b 5. d 6. d 7. b 8. d 9. d 10. c
11. c 12. d 13. b 14. a 15. c

ANSWER KEY

Chapter 11

1. d	2. d	3. d	4. b	5. d	6. d	7. d	8. b	9. a	10. d
11. d	12. c	13. b	14. c	15. d	16. d	17. a	18. c	19. a	20. a
21. a	22. b	23. d							

Chapter 12

1. a	2. b	3. d	4. b	5. d	6. b	7. d	8. d	9. d	10. a
11. c	12. c	13. b	14. a	15. d	16. d	17. b	18. c	19. d	20. d